THE CHICAGO GUIDE TO Fact-Checking

Permissions, A Survival Guide
Susan M. Bielstein

The Craft of Translation
John Biguenet and Rainer Schulte, editors

The Craft of Research
Wayne C. Booth, Gregory G. Colomb, Joseph M. Williams, Joseph Bizup, and William T. FitzGerald

Legal Writing in Plain English
Bryan A. Garner

Getting It Published
William Germano

Storycraft
Jack Hart

Cite Right
Charles Lipson

The Chicago Guide to Writing about Numbers
Jane E. Miller

The Chicago Guide to Communicating Science
Scott L. Montgomery

Indexing Books
Nancy C. Mulvany

Developmental Editing
Scott Norton

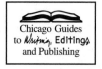

The Subversive Copy Editor
Carol Fisher Saller

The Chicago Guide to
FACT-CHECKING

Brooke Borel

THE UNIVERSITY OF CHICAGO PRESS Chicago and London

The University of Chicago Press, Chicago 60637
The University of Chicago Press, Ltd., London

Printed in the United States of America

25 24 23 22 21 20 19 18 17 16 1 2 3 4 5

ISBN-13: 978-0-226-29076-8 (cloth)
ISBN-13: 978-0-226-29093-5 (paper)
ISBN-13: 978-0-226-29109-3 (e-book)
DOI: 10.7208/chicago/9780226291093.001.0001

Library of Congress Cataloging-in-Publication Data

Names: Borel, Brooke, author.
Title: The Chicago guide to fact-checking / Brooke Borel.
Other titles: Chicago guides to writing, editing, and publishing.
Description: Chicago; London : The University of Chicago Press, 2016. | Series: Chicago guides to writing, editing, and publishing
Identifiers: LCCN 2016018060 | ISBN 9780226290768 (cloth: alk. paper) | ISBN 9780226290935 (pbk.: alk. paper) | ISBN 9780226291093 (e-book)
Subjects: LCSH: Research—Handbooks, manuals, etc. | Internet Research—Handbooks, manuals, etc.
Classification: LCC ZA3075 .B67 2016 | DDC 001.4/202854678—dc23 LC record available at https://lccn.loc.gov/2016018060

♾ This paper meets the requirements of ANSI/NISO Z39.48-1992 (Permanence of Paper).

Contents

Introduction

There's never been a better time to do a book about fact-checking. As I worked on this guide, dozens of people expressed this sentiment to me. It's a reasonable thought: in the year and a half between the project's conception and my completed first draft, we collectively witnessed the meltdown from *Rolling Stone*'s inaccurate story about a rape at a University of Virginia fraternity; the public humiliation of NBC's *Nightly News* anchor, Brian Williams, who spun tall tales about experiencing a rocket-propelled grenade attack while reporting in Iraq, among other things; and Google's foray into "estimating the trustworthiness of web sources." In early 2016, the editor in chief of the *Intercept*, an online magazine, wrote a note to readers about a "recently discovered pattern of deception in the actions of a staff member." One of the *Intercept*'s reporters, Juan Thompson, had fabricated quotes and impersonated people through fake e-mail accounts. Many other outlets had picked up Thompson's false reports, including the *New York Daily News, New York Post, New York Magazine, Root,* and the *Toronto Sun.*

But the idea that there has never been a better time to write an editorial fact-checking guide could just as easily apply to previous eras in journalism—or any nonfiction media, for that matter. In 2012 it was Jonah Lehrer, a wunderkind science writer who fabricated Bob Dylan quotes in his book *Imagine,* among other transgressions. In 2003 Jayson Blair was caught making up stories and plagiarizing while Judith Miller was publishing inaccurate articles about Saddam Hussein's capacity to build weapons of mass destruction, both while writing for the *New York Times*. In 1998 the Pulitzer finalist Patricia Smith admitted she made up sources to give her *Boston Globe* column a kick, and in the same year a young journalist named Stephen Glass was caught in many elaborate frauds, including making up entire stories, for the *New Republic* and other publications. And in 1981 it was Janet Cooke, who was caught having published a made-up story in the *Washington Post* about an eight-year-old heroin addict named Jimmy the previous year. We could probably go back in time to the birth of the printing press and beyond to find cringe-worthy examples of presumably truthful accounts gone awry.

Our current media climate, then, isn't any better or worse than its predecessors. I do think, however, that we can point to one key difference: the Internet has ushered in unprecedented amounts of published information at an astonishing rate, and that information is readily accessible to anyone who can get online. That doesn't mean the Internet is to blame for all our current fact-checking woes. Still, as publications move online—and other web-only outlets and self-publishing platforms launch seemingly daily—fact-checking is growing less common. There just isn't time or money to check every drop from the Internet fire hose. As *Gawker*'s then–editor in chief John Cook told the *New York Times* in 2013: "We are dealing with a volume of information that it is impossible to have the strict standards of accuracy that other institutions have."

Many would argue that the Internet eventually self-corrects as readers swarm the comment sections to point out errors. That's the claim, anyway. But some publications, including *Popular Science* and *Mic*, have decided to do away with comments entirely. Even on websites where the comments remain, are we to always trust the commenters? And shouldn't we try to get things right the first time regardless of the swift, and sometimes misguided, hammer of Internet justice?

In truth, no matter the era or the media—whether print or online or audio or video—fact-checking is relevant, and not only for flagrant examples of journalistic misconduct but also for smaller errors. Misspellings. Sloppy descriptions. Poor sourcing. If journalism is a cornerstone of democracy, then fact-checking is its building inspector, ensuring that the structure of a piece of writing is sound.

Unfortunately, the actual process of editorial fact-checking—that is, a reality check performed by an independent person who was not involved in a story's creation—is not always taught in journalism school. Sure, students learn how to be reporters, and their professors, one hopes, drill into their heads again and again the notion that facts need to be, well, facts. And not everyone who might need to know how to fact-check even goes to journalism school to begin with or has the opportunity to learn fact-checking skills on the job.

While there is some overlap between the responsibilities of writer, editor, and fact-checker, each also has a unique role in creating a story. Those roles can sometimes even be in conflict. The goal of any writer of nonfiction—whether you want to call that writer a journalist, a reporter, or something else entirely—is to build a story out of facts. The first step is to gather those facts, which may come from interviews, written reports, data sets, and more. The writer must sift through these facts and figure out how each connects, all while paying attention to the structure of their story. How should they introduce the reader to the information? How and where will they support each claim? If the story is a long narrative, what are the main threads and how will the writer braid them together? What is the conclusion of the story, and how will the writer pare it down to a pithy or insightful kicker? Then, from a blank computer screen or piece of paper, the writer must stitch their reporting into a cohesive piece.

An editor's job is to take that piece and see if the story flows well. Maybe, for example, the writer's structure is too complicated for a reader to follow, and the editor decides to streamline it by changing the opening scene and the order of the following sections—a convoluted piece that jumps forward and backward in time may become a straightforward, chronological account. The editor also looks for holes in the story, from a leap in logic to a missing piece of key information, and may send the writer to hunt for more facts to fill these in. Good editors, too, will push back on the writer if something sounds too good to be true or if the sourcing appears inadequate.

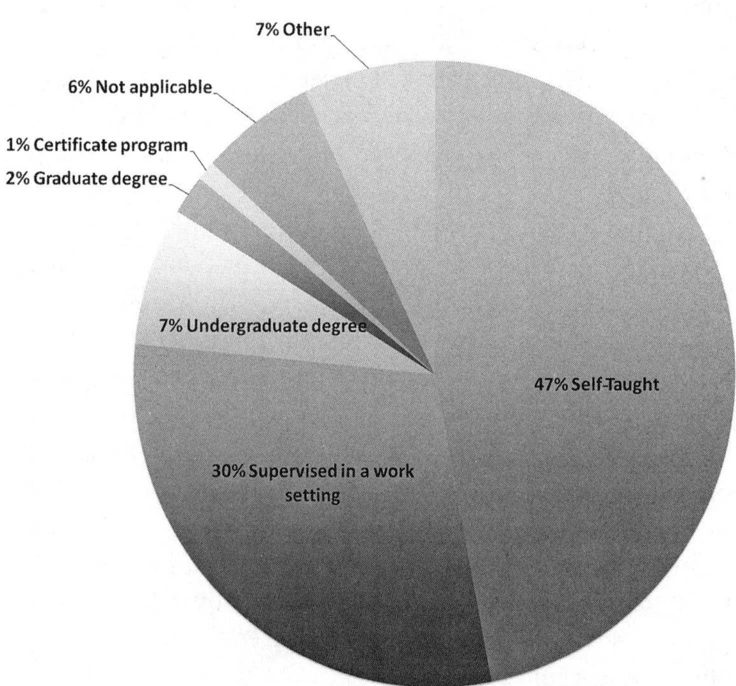

Figure 1. In my survey of 234 journalists from a range of media and specialties, nearly half said they learned to fact-check on their own and nearly a third were taught in a work setting. The survey data showed no clear indication that a degree or certificate in journalism had any impact on where the individual learned to fact-check.

After a story goes back and forth between a writer and editor, often many times, they get it into nearly final form. Then, ideally, it will land on the desk of a fact-checker. It is the fact-checker's job to unbraid the pieces of the story and examine each strand, testing its strength and probing for weak points; in the process, fact-checking also attempts to uncover whether any vital pieces of the story are missing. The fact-checker takes a hard look at the writer's sources to assess if they are trustworthy; decides whether the writer used the facts fairly and accurately to build the story; and pushes back against the writer and editor, who are now invested in the story and its structure, if the evidence doesn't support the way the story is written. "Even the best writing is really not good enough," says John Banta, the head of research (a term often used synonymously with fact-checking) at *Vanity Fair*, in describing in his job. "We provide a service where we go in and we take everything apart—we take the engine out of the car, throw the parts on the floor, and put it back together again."

There is certainly overlap in the skill sets required of a fact-checker and a writer. Learning how to fact-check can help writers become better reporters, because in a way fact-checking is reporting in reverse. Knowing how a fact-checker might pick a story apart helps a writer learn to think twice before relying on a questionable source. Writers also benefit from understanding the fact-checking process, even if they will never have the chance to do it themselves, particularly if they work for outlets that require it. Going through a fact-check is nerve-racking, but it also teaches writers to organize their source material and think about its quality: some outlets that use fact-checkers will require a writer to provide an annotated copy of their story that footnotes the sources they used for each and every fact. Knowing how to fact-check can also help writers when they are working for places that forgo the process. It's nearly impossible to truly fact-check one's own work—we tend to trust our judgment too much, assuming our reporting is solid even when it's shaky—but taking a step back from a piece and giving it the most critical read possible can save a writer from embarrassing mistakes.

There is also some overlap between the role of the fact-checker and the copy editor. Both may be concerned with issues such as the correct spelling of names, but copy editors are not responsible for verifying the broader factual accuracy of a story.

The fact-checking process happens at a range of media outlets, but it's most common at national magazines, where the trade has been passed down for decades apprenticeship-style. This may be because magazines have both the money and the time to invest in fact-checking, particularly compared to newspapers or nightly news shows, which are ephemeral, a flash that is replaced the next day by new stories or updates. And because the daily news cycle happens so quickly, particularly in the Internet age where it's updated minute by minute, the chance for correction comes ever more quickly. Magazine editors, on the other hand, may have to wait a month or two in order to print a correction, and so it's especially helpful to them to employ fact-checkers to get it right the first time around.

Some magazines still have fact-checkers on staff, while others hire freelancers. Checkers may also find work in other media such as radio shows and television documentaries. Some book authors also hire fact-checkers, since publishers don't typically provide the service, and many writers fact-check their own work despite the pitfalls of this practice. The relationship among writer, editor, and fact-checker described above can vary a bit in these different contexts.

Because the fact-checking tradition is most common to the magazine world, that particular process will serve as a model for much of this book, although I will also explore variations in other media. Even within the magazine world, however, it's useful to know that each publication has its own devices and

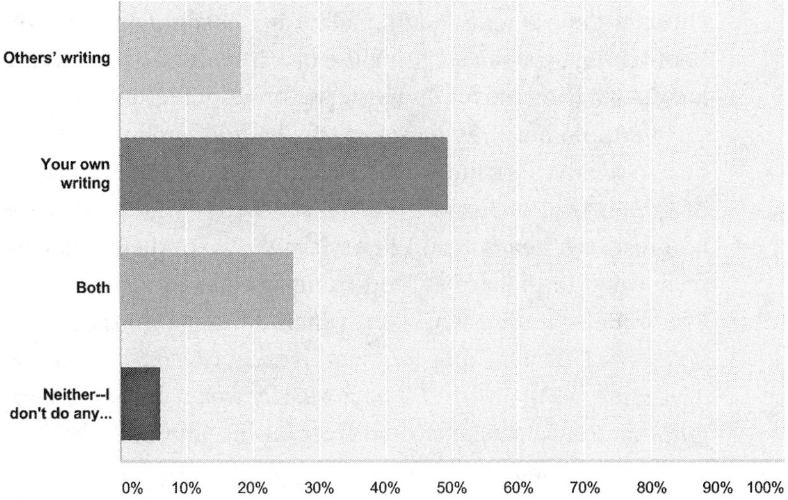

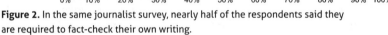

Figure 2. In the same journalist survey, nearly half of the respondents said they are required to fact-check their own writing.

requirements, although the overarching steps are largely the same. This book attempts to pull from the knowledge of magazine fact-checkers—as well as a handful who check radio shows, documentaries, news programs, and books—to bring the art of the fact-check from the magazine apprenticeship to you.

| | |

The advice presented in this book draws heavily from firsthand experience. My first job in journalism, which served as my J-school, was as a fact-checker and, later, a research editor at a magazine called *Science Illustrated*—an unusual fact-checking experience, as the magazine publishes in Danish and, during my tenure, was translated into English and then fact-checked and repackaged for an American audience. I've also worked as a fact-checker at *Quanta Magazine*, an online publication that features pieces about complex science and mathematics. For the past several years, I've also taught courses on fact-checking to writers and others interested in learning this skill and have consulted with publications starting new fact-checking departments. Additionally, I fact-checked my first nonfiction book, although I think the task is truly better off in the hands of a third party whenever possible.

To supplement my own experience and widen the range of perspectives included in the book, I conducted a survey of 234 current or former journalists, writers, fact-checkers, and research heads, and I interviewed 91 experts (some who responded to the survey, and some whom I found later on). The outlets they've worked for include the *Atlantic*, *Audubon*, CBS, *Discover*, *Entertainment Weekly*, *GQ*, *InStyle*, *Laptop Magazine*, *Men's Journal*, *More*, *Mother Jones*, *National Geographic*, the *Nation*, National Geographic Channel, the *New Republic*, the *New York Times Magazine*, the *New Yorker*, *Outside*, *Playboy*, *Popular Mechanics*, *Popular Science*, *Radiolab*, Retro Report, *Saveur*, the Smithsonian Channel, *Der Spiegel*, *Sports Illustrated*, *This American Life*, *Time*, *Vanity Fair*, *Vice*, the *Village Voice*, *Vogue*, and *Wired*. Some of the checkers have also worked on best-selling nonfiction books. Their tales from the field appear throughout the book, and their advice informs my discussion even where it isn't specifically quoted.

A caveat: Although its very name implies a rigid objectivity, fact-checking is rarely cut-and-dried. Truths and facts can be more slippery than you think, particularly when you move from the basics, like the spelling of a person's name, to the fuzzier realms of argument building or narrative pacing. Fact-checking, too, is not a static practice, but one that changes not only with the times but from one publication to another and even from one type of story to another. The level of reporting in a celebrity profile, for example, doesn't have the same expectations as an in-depth investigative piece, and the accompanying reality check is similarly different. And so, you may find checkers who disagree with portions of this book—surely even among the people I've interviewed.

Being a fact-checker is often humbling in the face of the unattainable task of finding and confirming facts and then deciding whether they've built something true, particularly when even that seemingly objective term simply isn't actually solid at all. Whose truth? Whose perception of reality? "Fact" and "truth" may seem synonymous, but the words are distinct. A fact is something you can't argue your way out of, like the dimensions of this page you're reading or the fact that this sentence started with the words "a fact." Truth is a fact or set of facts in context: knowing the dimensions of the page and the words on it doesn't convey the information on the pages, or the order in which I've placed the facts to make my point.

In other words, while the facts are indisputable, the truth a writer builds from them is a matter of interpretation. Even if the facts don't change, the order in which you place them can shift the meaning of a piece: give two journalists the same assignment, and each will write an entirely different story. Give them identical source material to build their story, and each may still come up with something unique. But despite these challenges, a good fact-checker forges on with obsessiveness, aiming for truth even when it is impossible, stubbornly questioning those words on the page, and holding them up to every possible light.

Because of these and other obstacles to uncovering facts and truth, you will certainly find that even the best and most thoroughly fact-checked writing has errors or fudges. There are a couple of key reasons why. First, a story that includes a fact-checker's every hedge, clarification, and lengthy contextual explanation turns into an unreadable snoozer. Knowing how to get the information right while keeping the heart and soul of a story—and yes, its truth—intact is an art. Second, writers and checkers are only human, and with that come inevitable failures. We're complex creatures with messy psychologies and faulty memories. In every story we write or edit or fact-check, we are dealing with deadlines, interpersonal politics, and our own unavoidable biases. As such, the examples of mistakes or corrections I use in this book aren't intended to shame those who made them, but to serve as a warning of what can go wrong even in the best publications with the best intentions.

Even this guide will have errors—at least from someone's perspective or interpretation—despite the surreal meta-experience of hiring a fact-checker to fact-check a fact-checking book, and I cringe in anticipation at the delight that readers will surely take in pointing out my own errors for years to come. (*Aren't you the person who wrote the fact-checking book? Shouldn't you always get everything right?!*).

Well, it's more complicated than that. Through this book, I hope to show you why. I also hope to convince you why—despite the attempts of researchers from Indiana University, Bloomington, who have developed an algorithm that can figure out the accuracy of simple trivia questions—the fact-checking robots of the future are not yet upon us. The best fact-checkers are still mere humans.

| | |

This book is a hybrid: part guide, to help you work as a fact-checker or attempt to check your own writing, and part overview of fact-checking in today's media, to offer context for the settings in which the work of checking takes place.

Chapter 1: "Why We Fact-Check" offers a more thorough explanation of the underlying need for fact-checking than you've experienced in these short introductory pages. The chapter will also provide cautionary tales where fact-checking or reporting went wrong, as well as what a fact-checker might look for to prevent similar debacles from happening under their watch. Here, I'll also go through some of the legal implications for getting facts wrong.

The short answer to the question posed in Chapter 2: "What We Fact-Check" is "everything." But it isn't enough to say that and expect someone to know what that actually entails. This chapter lays out the sorts of information that a fact-checker should check. Beginning in this chapter, you'll find occasional "Think Like a Fact-Checker" sections that invite you to try your hand at some fact-checking skills. The questions are open-ended, and there are no answers provided, but the goal is to encourage reflection on the issues raised and let you experience the complexity of what it means to fact-check.

Chapter 3: "How We Fact-Check" gets into the process of fact-checking. This chapter is a good reference for when you are new to fact-checking and you aren't sure where to start or how to keep track of the facts in a story (or how to get along with your editor or writer). I use the magazine fact-check as a model, but I will also show how this approach can be applied to other media including television and radio, both of which have unique considerations. And while fact-checking your own work is seen as impossible by many folks, this chapter also provides tips on how to double-check your own story if you are working without a fact-checker. Here you will also begin encountering boxed features labeled "Quick Guide," which summarize key sections of the text for easy reference, and "Pro Tip," which offer more detailed or specialized information on issues discussed in the text.

While the previous chapter walks you through the process, Chapter 4: "Checking Different Types of Facts" is a reference guide that explains how to check specific categories of facts, from descriptions to statistics to summaries of a scientific study.

The quality of a fact-check depends on the quality of the source materials. Chapter 5: "Sourcing" explains the difference between primary and secondary sources and explores how to judge a source, whether it is one that you've found on your own or something a writer has offered in their backup material for a piece. The chapter also provides advice on how to contact people who are sources, as well as how to interact with them.

Chapter 6: "Record Keeping" asks: What do you do with all your sources and story drafts after a story has published? This brief chapter offers suggestions on how to organize and store your documents, and explains why this is important both from a legal and practical perspective.

In Chapter 7: "Test Your Skills," you can try your hand at fact-checking a short piece of writing. Note, though, that this particular piece is just one of many types of writing you might encounter as a fact-checker, and both the format and the sourcing aren't as intricate as you would find in a narrative feature, an investigative piece, or other more complex stories. The answer key appears in appendix 1, but keep in mind that the sources listed there are just examples—the piece could have been written just as well using other source materials—and don't cheat!

The conclusion offers some final thoughts about fact-checking in a world where so much of the news and other nonfiction media we consume is online, where standards are murky, though perhaps getting clearer.

After all this, want to learn more about fact-checking? Appendix 2 recommends additional books, articles, and radio programs on the topic.

ONE ||| Why We Fact-Check

When writers present a piece as nonfiction, they create a contract with the reader. This is true whether the piece in question is a newspaper article, a magazine feature, or the script for a documentary. The writer is saying *this happened.* To bolster their account, they present evidence including, though certainly not limited to, quotes from experts, data, and eyewitness reports. Together, these sources give the story a foundation. The overarching argument that the writer builds on top of this foundation is important, too: it tells the reader *not only did this happen,* but *here is the context in which you should consider what happened.*

But somewhere between all the reading, interviewing, and thinking, the foundation may crack and crumble. Maybe the problem is minimal—a simple misunderstanding or copy error, like flubbing a person's official title or inadvertently transposing the digits in a number. If the crack is small and the remaining sources are solid, the story could survive. Still, it's a crack, and an observant reader starts to wonder about the rest of the structure. Take, for example, a 2012 *Vogue* profile of Chelsea Clinton in which Daniel Baer, who at the time was the Deputy Assistant Secretary for the Bureau of Democracy, Human Rights, and Labor at the U.S. Department of State, was identified as an interior designer. At its surface, flubbing a job title is a relatively small misunderstanding. But knowing this particular flub, do you trust the rest of the story?

Then there are the more glaring problems that shake a story's foundation: explanations oversimplified to the point that they are wrong, credulous sources, and gross misunderstandings of an event and its context. Take, for example, the 2012 Supreme Court ruling on the Affordable Care Act, when both CNN and Fox News briefly reported that a controversial and key piece—the individual mandate—had been struck when in fact it had not. Or consider a 2015 article by *New York Times* tech writer Nick Bilton, which suggested that wearable technologies are as bad for your health as smoking cigarettes. Science writers criticized the story, pointing out that Bilton cherry-picked a handful of studies that tried to link cell phones to cancer—ignoring a swath of research that said otherwise—and also quoted a controversial alternative medicine proponent as an expert. The mistake ultimately resulted in a response from the newspaper's public editor, Margaret Sullivan, and the online version later included a 200-word addendum.

Even worse are full-blown earthquakes where the writer commits plagiarism or publishes outright alterations or fabrications of quotes, or other lies. For examples of journalistic misconduct, look no further than Jayson Blair, who plagiarized and fabricated stories for the *New York Times* including a series on the Washington Sniper in 2002; Patricia Smith, who fabricated pieces of her *Boston Globe* column; Jonah Lehrer, who self-plagiarized several posts for the *New Yorker* blog and also made up several Bob Dylan quotes in his book *Imagine*; Stephen Glass, who not only fabricated stories but also his fact-checking notes and sources while working for the *New Republic*; Judith Miller, who relied on inaccurate sources in her coverage leading up to the Iraq War; or Michael Finkel, who made up a composite character, along with other fabrications, for a *New York Times Magazine* profile in 2002. All of these writers committed these sins in order to tell a good yarn or make a persuasive argument.

In other cases, writers may twist the ground rules with a source in order to use or attribute material that wasn't agreed upon. Usually, writers and their sources will be clear about whether the source's comments are on the record, which means their identity may be included in the story, or on background, in which it may not (for definitions and further discussion, see chapter 4). Writers should honor these and other rules of source attribution, but a look at their interview notes and recordings may reveal that they, in fact, have not.

There are also grayer areas that fall between simple errors or intentional rule breaking. A writer's own biases may sneak into the work. Writers and editors, too, while crafting a compelling and page-turning narrative, may shuffle a few facts to help with the story's flow. And when a writer has spent weeks, months, or even years on a piece, it is difficult, if not impossible, to step outside to catch these mistakes. A blind spot will probably continue to be a blind spot. Further, each newspaper, book publisher, magazine, podcast, and more has a unique worldview and the stories it shares will reflect that, which adds another layer of perspective and spin on how a story is told.

Independent fact-checkers—people who are not involved in the story's creation—temper these gray areas and catch the more obvious and easy mistakes. "Fact-checkers, we're like the janitors, the custodians. We clean up after everybody," says Beatrice Hogan, the former research chief at *More* magazine. Indeed, a good fact-checker goes through a story both word by word and from a big-picture view, zooming in to examine each individual fact or statement and then zooming out to see whether the story's premise is sound. The fact-checker's presence does not absolve the writer and the editor from their mistakes; the responsibility is on everyone to deliver the most accurate story possible. Still, the fact-checker will likely feel the weight of a mistake the most, particularly if it was an oversight on their part or the insertion of an error where there was none before, and not an error the team made collectively. The fact-checker is indeed like a janitor, but an especially meticulous and skeptical one.

It's also worth noting that a fact-checking department is only as good as its media outlet allows it to be. If everyone involved in a story, from the writer to the editors to the art department, respects the craft of fact-checking, this support only furthers the cause. If the staff doesn't care for the fact-checking process, or if checkers feel that they can't speak up when they see a story's foundation crumbling, the entire process is doomed.

Fact-checking is also important when it comes to the Internet, both in using online sources and consuming online media. This is particularly true in an age where hoaxes make it into national news reports unchecked. There is nothing inherently bad about online information, and it isn't necessarily unique from a historical perspective. Hoaxes, sensationalism, and other wildly inaccurate accounts were around long before we went digital. Take, for example, the Winsted Wildman of Connecticut, an old Bigfoot hoax, or the yellow journalism of the 1890s, like the time William Randolph Hearst used his newspapers to fan the flames of the Spanish-American War.

"I very much reject the idea that the Internet is full of errors any more than print," says Adrienne LaFrance, a senior editor at the *Atlantic*, who used to run a column at *Gawker* called "Antiviral," where she debunked fake online stories. "I think the major difference now versus the pre-Internet is that everyone is a publisher, but not everyone has to stake their professional reputation on accuracy."

Indeed, there are two key differences between the past and the present. The first, as LaFrance points out, is that the digital age made it possible for virtually anyone with an Internet connection to publish their writing. As such, we circulate a glut of information daily—some of it great, some mediocre, and some terrible. While this has democratized journalism and publishing, making it more accessible to people who previously weren't able to participate in it, it's also led to a virtual avalanche that is hard to sift. Second, we are able to amplify any of these stories by effectively republishing them on Twitter, Facebook, Tumblr, and a slew of other social media platforms. It's so easy to click a headline and then click again to like or Tweet or reblog it, that we're collectively bombarded with inaccurate stories—whether intentionally so or because of honest mistakes.

Internet fact failures take many forms. In one category, legacy news outlets and newer media sites alike post stories without fact-checking them, essentially publishing hoaxes as news. This phenomenon is, in part, an unfortunate result of aggregation, in which online outlets pick up stories from one another without adding any original reporting. Take this example from 2013, when bored Americans celebrating Thanksgiving were riveted by a drama unfolding on several news websites. A man named Elan Gale was live-Tweeting an apparent feud with a woman named Diane on a US Airways flight. Gale claimed he had seen Diane act rudely to a flight attendant and proceeded to send her alcoholic drinks and notes essentially telling her to lighten up. She wrote back. Gale took photos of the notes and broadcast the images to his Twitter followers, which ballooned from a reported 35,000 to 140,000 following the exchange. The story hit its climax after the plane landed, when Diane approached Gale in the airport and slapped him. Many news outlets picked up the story, including ABC, Business Insider, BuzzFeed, CBC, Fox, and the *New York Daily News*.

But the story wasn't true. Gale—who had previously mostly posted jokes on Twitter—made it up in order to entertain his followers during the holiday travel. In a follow-up interview with ABC, Gale reportedly said of the initial media coverage: "My thought was I can't believe anyone is taking this seriously. I thought, 'Why isn't anyone doing any fact checking?' Then I saw it was on the evening news in Sacramento and it became this totally absurd thing."

Publishing a hoax weakens readers' trust in an outlet's ability to report the news, which is a problem on its own. But publishing incorrect information in more dire circumstances has even more harmful consequences. Take the media frenzy during Hurricane Sandy in 2012, the Boston Marathon bombing in 2013, or any other catastrophic event that has unfolded in the age of social media. In these cases especially, outlets are under pressure to publish—and publish fast. And it means that a lot of that published information ends up being wrong. During Hurricane Sandy, for example, Reuters picked up a rumor circulating on Twitter that nineteen Con Edison workers were trapped in a power station, surely an upsetting report for anyone with family or friends who work for the utility. And after the Boston Marathon bombing, reporters from outlets including CBS and BuzzFeed retweeted a message that said: "Police on scanner identify the names of #BostonMarathon suspects in gunfight, Suspect 1: Mike Mulugeta. Suspect 2: Sunil Tripathi." The trouble was neither man was actually a suspect, and there is no evidence that the Boston police even mentioned the latter's name. Tripathi, a Brown University student, not only had nothing to do with the bombing—he had been missing for a month and his family had been frantically searching for him. The false accusations were painful on their own, but, worse, he was later found dead from an apparent, and unrelated, suicide.

Another case where the pressure to publish breaking news played an unfortunate role was in the aftermath of a 2011 shooting in Tucson, Arizona, where a gunman opened fire on a crowd, hitting eighteen people, including U.S. Representative Gabrielle Giffords. Six people died. Early reports claimed Giffords was one of them, from outlets including CBS, CNN, Fox, the *Huffington Post*, the *New York Times*, NPR, and Reuters. In fact, Giffords wasn't dead but had been shot in the head and was rushed into surgery. The false news and Twitter announcements made an already frightening and sobering situation all the more difficult for Representative Giffords's family and constituents, as well as the nation as a whole.

A year after the Arizona shooting, Craig Silverman—who at the time covered errors, corrections, fact-checking, and

NPR News
@nprmews
Following
BREAKING: Rep. Giffords (D-AZ), 6 others killed by gunman in Tucson http://n.pr/fjnZW5
RETWEETS 592
FAVORITES 18
1:12 PM - 8 Jan 2011

Figure 3. NPR News was one of many outlets that falsely reported the death of Representative Gabrielle Giffords in the aftermath of a chaotic shooting.

verification at the *Poynter* blog "Regret the Error" and has a book by the same name—recounted the debacle: "Twitter gave me a window into the captivating mixture of urgency, confusion and information that emerges when major news breaks and the story takes off." Indeed, this process used to happen in the newsroom as reporters decided how and when to report breaking news. In the Internet era, the often-messy aspects are aired in the open, which is unfortunate because this is where readers can access the information and assume it is true. As Silverman notes in the same post, local Arizona news outlets got the Giffords story right. This provides insight on how to judge news when you're Tweeting from a distance: look for publications as geographically close to the story as possible, because they have the best vantage point (for more tips, see Silverman's *Verification Handbook: A Definitive Guide to Verifying Digital Content for Emergency Coverage*.)

Most breaking-news outlets don't employ independent fact-checkers, partly because of time constraints; television and web reporters who are covering these sorts of stories have to rely on their own sourcing because they're on short deadline. Still, examining where stories like this can go wrong is instructive: look for the potential weak spots to see how you would have checked it, if you had the opportunity. In the Gale Thanksgiving hoax, a fact-checker might have confirmed the story not just with Gale, but also with the airline and, if possible, "Diane." In the stories about Hurricane Sandy, the Boston Marathon, and the Arizona shooting, a checker should know that a rumor circulating on Twitter must be confirmed before it is repeated or put in a story—this could have been accomplished through a phone call to Con Ed or to the Boston Police Department or to the hospital, respectively.

Beyond these philosophical and practical reasons for fact-checking, there are also the legal incentives. If a story is wrong, it damages not only the writer's reputation but also that of the publisher, particularly for controversial or investigative pieces where the stakes are high. Factual errors may open an outlet to lawsuits, which can run into damages worth millions of dollars. Fact-checkers should be aware of several areas of law—including defamation, copyright, and invasion of privacy—and be especially vigilant with relevant sources. Necessary disclaimer: What follows is not intended as legal advice. If you're unsure about whether your work opens you or your publication to lawsuits, consult an attorney.

Defamation comes in two flavors: slander, which is spoken, and libel, which is written (although, confusingly, defamation in news broadcasts and the like is usually considered libel). In either case, defamation involves making a false statement about a person or company—one that is done so with fault and damages a reputation. Usually, a plaintiff—the person bringing the suit—has to prove the information was indeed inaccurate and that it harmed them in some tangible way, such as losing a job or anything else that can be connected to money (although the injury could also be the emotional stress that results from a damaged reputation).

Defamation laws are different for public and private citizens. Public figures include celebrities, government officials, politicians, and more, all of whom lose some of their expectations for privacy when they enter the public sphere. In order to successfully sue for defamation, a public figure must prove that the information was published or spoken with actual malice. This doesn't mean the publisher or speaker harbored actual ill will against the public figure, but that they knew the information was incorrect and published it anyway. It's up to the plaintiff to prove actual malice.

In 2011 former Chicago Bulls player Scottie Pippen sued NBC Universal Media LLC and CBS Interactive Inc. because of an inaccurate story that suggested he had filed for bankruptcy. But although the reporter had documentation proving a Scottie Pippen had declared bankruptcy, it turned out that it was not the basketball player but a different man. The U.S. Supreme Court ultimately declined to hear the case while a lower court dismissed it, because Pippen could not prove that the publications knew they had the wrong person and thus had no evidence of actual malice. Even though the case was dismissed, it would have been better to avoid it to begin with. If faced with a story like this, a fact-checker would want better confirmation that the Scottie Pippen on the bankruptcy documents was indeed the basketball player, perhaps by comparing addresses and other identifying information in those documents, or contacting the athlete through his booking agent or other representative.

The court case that established actual malice in public figure defamation is a famous one, and it's worth mentioning: *New York Times Co. v. L. B. Sullivan*, which went before the U.S. Supreme Court in 1964. L. B. Sullivan, the public safety commissioner in Montgomery, Alabama, sued the *Times* for libel in state court after the paper published an advertisement seeking money to defend Martin Luther King Jr. in a 1960 indictment. The ad included a few errors—it said, for example, that Alabama police had arrested King seven times, when it had been four—and although Sullivan wasn't specifically named, he felt the information was defamatory. An Alabama state court awarded him half a million dollars. But the case got bumped to the Supreme Court, which unanimously ruled for the newspaper. Under the First and Fourteenth Amendments, the court said, a state can't award damages to public figures unless they can prove actual malice, defined as a statement "made with knowledge of its falsity or with reckless disregard of whether it was true or false." Despite the outcome, this case underscores the importance of checking even seemingly small facts, like the number of times an event happened—in this case, King's arrests.

In another famous libel case, this one starting in 1984 and lasting a decade, the psychoanalyst Jeffrey Masson sued the *New Yorker* and affiliates for $10 million after Janet Malcolm, a freelancer at the magazine, wrote a lengthy and juicy profile about him. The suit alleged that Malcolm had fabricated quotes and other information and, at one point during the long case, pulled the fact-checker into the conversation. Masson said he had raised points of inaccuracy with the checker, Nancy Franklin, and that she had brushed him off. In one of many rulings, an appeals court that sent the case back to a trial jury suggested that because the *New Yorker* employed a fact-checking process that uncovered questions about some of the details in Malcolm's article, the magazine was open to greater scrutiny than if it had no process. Ultimately, the court let Malcolm off the hook, concluding that although the quotes might be false, they needed more evidence to prove it. The *New Yorker* has a famously robust fact-checking team, so it's hard to know whether there was something more Franklin could have done, particularly in this case, where the subject of a negative story had so much incentive to sue. It's still a good reminder that as a fact-checker, your work may be scrutinized by a court.

The law shields private figures from the public eye, which makes it easier to prove defamation. Specifically, private individuals only have to prove that a publisher or broadcaster was negligent, meaning they failed to follow the reasonable journalistic steps required to figure out if a piece of information is true or false. Of course, private individuals still have to prove that the statement was indeed false and that it caused them injury. The key Supreme Court case establishing rules for private figures is *Gertz v. Robert Welch, Inc.* in which a lawyer, Elmer Gertz, sued Robert Welch, the owner of the John Birch Society's *American Opinion*. The publication had run a story in 1969 about a Chicago police officer who had shot a man dead and was subsequently convicted of second-degree murder. Gertz had represented the dead man's family in a separate civil case, and *American Opinion* claimed that the lawyer was a "communist-fronter" and "Leninist," among other things. Welch tried to invoke *New York Times v. Sullivan*, but the Supreme Court's decision pointed out that Gertz was a private individual and therefore had greater protection against defamation. For any fact-checker, it is important to consider whether a person in a story is a public or private figure, particularly if that person is depicted in a negative light, and take extra care in fact-checking such claims.

Defamation laws vary greatly from one country to another. In the United Kingdom, for example, it is far easier to sue for slander or libel than in the United States. In one famous case that began in 2008, the writer Simon Singh published a column in the *Guardian* criticizing chiropractic therapy, an alternative medicine. The British Chiropractic Association sued Singh, and a court battle ensued that lasted two years. Eventually the BCA withdrew their suit. Still, all writers and fact-checkers should be aware of defamation laws in the countries in which their stories will appear.

Unlike defamation, invasion of privacy can include statements that are true. The definition here is knotty, but it basically means that a person is allowed a reasonable expectation of privacy. A reporter or publication, for example, can't record someone in their home without their knowledge or consent and then publish quotes or other information that came from those recordings. Publications often can't reveal intimate or private facts such as sexual practices or particularly sensitive illnesses, or use a person's name or likeness without their permission. In one famous invasion of privacy case, the father of a soldier who died in Iraq sued *Harper's Magazine* for publishing a photograph from the soldier's open-casket funeral. An Oklahoma district court sided with the photographer and *Harper's* because the funeral was public and the story was a matter of public interest. Had the photograph shown a private citizen at a closed funeral, however, the case may have had legs. These are the sorts of details a fact-checker should confirm.

There is also the matter of copyright infringement, in which an author uses intellectual property that belongs to someone else without permission. This may include not only text, but also images, song lyrics, music, audio, or video. The responsibility for most of these cases will fall to either the editorial team or the art department, but it's still helpful for the fact-checker to be aware of the rules and look out for possible slips. (Copyright infringement shouldn't be confused with plagiarism. According to Rob Bertsche, a media attorney at Prince Lobel Tye LLP in Boston, the former is the unapproved use of someone's creative expression while the latter is use without attribution.)

For journalists, there are important exceptions from copyright infringement: ideas and facts. These are free and legal for *anyone* to use; it's *how* the ideas are expressed that is protected by copyright. In other words, you can use the same basic facts as another writer, but you can't imitate how that writer presents those facts. And in some cases, even the use of a specific expression may be defended by what is called fair use, a complicated calculus that may determine that the use of the material is allowed.

Such legal matters may be hard for the layperson to parse, and so some publications employ a media-savvy lawyer to look over stories before they publish. The lawyer will typically go through any potentially damaging statements and ask how they were sourced, possibly requesting to see the backup material. If the sourcing is sound but the wording still opens the publication to suit, the lawyer may suggest changes to the text that offer better protection. A fact-checker isn't the only person responsible for bringing potential legal problems to the lawyer's attention—this mainly falls to the editors and research directors—but a fact-checker should still be familiar with media ethics and look out for potentially damning statements.

With all this in mind, why isn't fact-checking more common in the media? Part of the reason, as already noted, is that it simply isn't possible in fast-paced daily newsrooms or on 24-hour news cycles. For many online publications, which often pay writers less compared to print magazines, there isn't a budget for a fact-checking team. "It's heartbreaking to see fact-checking get treated like an outmoded luxury that old-fashioned journalism indulged in along with three martini lunches," says Carl Zimmer, a science writer and columnist for the *New York Times* who worked as a fact-checker for *Discover* magazine early in his career. "I understand that online journalism has to be a torrent of words to succeed financially, but allowing material to flow online without checking it corrupts our shared understanding of the history we're living."

Fact-checking shouldn't be a luxury in journalism or any work of nonfiction. But as traditional publications juggle budgets for fact-checking staff, or do with fewer checkers on tighter schedules, and new publications fail to incorporate fact-checking into their routines, the process could face extinction across media. Still, it's not all bleak. There are many publications that care a great deal about fact-checking, from *Der Spiegel,* a weekly magazine in Germany that at one point employed an astonishing seventy fact-checkers, to many national magazines across the United States. Independent fact-checking is working its way into other media, too, from documentary films put out by the National Geographic Channel to radio shows including *This American Life* and *Radiolab* to the new documentary publisher Retro Report. Even the comedy news show *Last Week Tonight with John Oliver* employs news researchers to double-check its segments. Outlets that don't go through a full fact-check often require backup materials from their writers, too, and an editor will look through these materials to make sure that the sources are sound.

Writers can also apply the tools of fact-checking to their own work. While it isn't a perfect solution, it is at least a chance to ask: Did this happen the way I think it happened? Why do I think so? Where did I find each of these facts, and are my sources trustworthy? And ultimately: How do I know this is true?

TWO ||| What We Fact-Check

The opening scenes of the short film *FCU: Fact Checkers Unit,* a 2008 Sundance Film Festival selection, will be familiar and funny to most fact-checkers. In the scene, an editor at the fictional *Dictum* magazine played by Kristen Schaal, stands over a team of two fact-checkers played by Peter Karinen and Brian Sacca. The checkers fly through a list of facts she's assigned to them, finish, and proudly hand her their report.

"Oh, you missed one," she says, pointing to a piece of paper that has fallen on the floor.

One of the checkers picks it up and reads aloud:

"Celebrity sleeping tips: If you're having trouble sleeping, just drink a glass of warm milk before you go to bed, like Bill Murray."

"Where did they find that?" the other checker asks.

"I think Wikipedia," the editor says.

In a panic, the checkers sputter:

"That is a user-generated site!"

"That could have been written by a seven-year-old!"

"I think we're gonna need some time on this one."

Instead, the editor gives them the near-impossible deadline of *tomorrow*. The checkers pray to a portrait of Alex Trebek of *Jeopardy!* fame and then—spoiler alert—set to work, ultimately tracking down Murray's address, breaking into his apartment, and getting caught once they're there. Instead of kicking the fact-checkers out, Murray asks them to stay, and in a montage that flits through several hours, the trio watches *M*A*S*H,* drinks martinis, reads, plays checkers and catch, and jams out an interpretive version of chopsticks at the piano. Then, just after midnight, Murray yawns and one of the checkers pours him a glass of warm 2 percent milk. As the checkers watch him drift to sleep in his bed, they say to one another: "Fact, checked."

It's a silly example, but the film's exaggeration hints at the great lengths a checker may take in order to prove a fact. Of course in the real world, a phone call with Bill Murray's publicist, or at the very least some solid secondary sourcing, such as an interview in which he discloses his love for warm milk before bed, would be preferable to breaking and entering. But traveling great distances to a source isn't necessarily outlandish for a fact-checker. Cynthia Cotts, a journalist and researcher with more than twenty-five years in the business, recalls an all-expenses-paid trip from New York to Los Angeles to access source materials for a *New Yorker* story in 1995. The story was an excerpt from Norman Mailer's book *Oswald's Tale: An American Mystery*, which covered, among other things, Lee Harvey Oswald's experiences in the Soviet Union. The source material was at the home of Mailer's colleague, the movie producer Lawrence Schiller, who didn't want the papers to leave his sight because they had been difficult to procure. And so Cotts and a colleague traveled to Schiller and spent three or four days sifting through original documents, including pieces from the Russian intelligence agencies.

Comedy and intrigue aside, when a fact-checker asks what they need to check, the answer is: everything. Even if the fact is a celebrity's sleep tips, and especially if the original source came from Wikipedia or any other source compiled by anonymous sources (for more on sourcing, including when and how Wikipedia is useful, see chapter 4).

What is *everything*? To give a non-exhaustive list of examples:

- The spelling of names and places
- Physical descriptions of people, places, and things
- Dates
- Ages

- Quotes
- Numbers
- Measurements and conversions
- Geographic locations and descriptions
- Scientific or technical explanations
- Titles, job descriptions, and affiliations
- Details about products including prices, specifications, and descriptions
- Quotes from movies or other well-known media
- Historical quotes or stories, even those that are widely assumed to be true
- Illustrations and photos, including the captions
- Definitions and word choices
- Overarching arguments
- Even the thing you just checked last week
- Even things you think you know are true

This last category—things you think you already know are true—is especially difficult, because it's tempting to skip familiar information. A thorough checker does not give in to this temptation, according to Corinne Cummings, who has worked as a fact-checker for *Rolling Stone* and *Playboy*. "One thing I do think that fact-checkers should keep in mind is to be more sensitive when you know a subject well," she says. "That is when you can get caught up in reading and think: *Of course I know that that's true.*" One way to get around your own knowledge bias is to force yourself to identify a source for each fact, whether that source comes from the writer or from your own research. You'll need this documentation for your records, anyway, so you might as well read it carefully and make sure whatever knowledge you think you have is indeed correct.

Finally, a good checker must also look for what is missing from the story. Are there any possible sources or perspectives that, by omission, make the story wrong? The best checkers will doggedly pursue each fact as well as these gaps, and those who try the hardest and longest to confirm each piece of information are those who will be the most successful at the job. It isn't a matter of being a genius researcher, but of being tireless and resourceful.

While each individual fact may be relatively easy to identify as something the checker needs to confirm, there are also the grayer areas discussed in the previous chapter—the arguments that stand on the writer's fact-based foundation. As a checker, it is vital that you consider these, too, no matter how difficult. "We should constantly ask questions of ourselves, of the journalist, and of the expert: How do you know this? How are you in a position to know this? Were you there when it happened? Did you talk to people who were there?" says Yvonne Rolzhausen, the head of the fact-checking department at the *Atlantic*. "You constantly turn over those stones to say 'why,' and if you continue to do that, you will ultimately be fine in terms of checking. In my mind, checking is such a combination of the small and the large—the trees and the forest. Do all of the trees match up to the forest? So if every fact is a tree, if you start lopping off the trees left, right, and center, do you still have a forest?"

To identify which pieces of a story are facts and need to be confirmed, a fact-checker must be diligent, patient, and tenacious. If you're unsure whether a specific part of a story is a fact, think about what steps you would need to do in order to confirm it. If those steps exist, it goes on the fact-checking list.

Think Like a Fact-Checker

When you finish this chapter, get a pencil or pen and then read it again. Underline the facts that you would check if you were fact-checking these pages.

Now let's go back to the fictional Bill Murray example in *FCU: Fact Checkers Unit*. If you were fact-checking this in real life, how would you do it? If the checker literally hands Murray a glass of warm milk and then puts the actor to bed, does that truly show us that this is something Murray would have done otherwise? Just as important as identifying each fact, if not more so, is *how* a checker proceeds through the fact-check—and whether those facts really amount to the truth.

THREE ||| How We Fact-Check

Now that you understand the why and the what, *how* exactly do you fact-check? Most professional checkers follow a series of steps that are either laid out by their boss or self-designed. The details vary, but the basic mechanics follow a similar blueprint from one outlet to the next. It's a long, tedious process—and yes, you may not always have time to do as thorough a job as you'd like. But here is how a full fact-check would happen. This is a general description of the process, using the magazine fact-check as a model and then addressing other media after. Details on how to check certain types of facts, as well as how to source those facts, appear in the following chapters.

Where fact-checkers fit in the editorial scheme differs from one outlet to the next. In some cases, a research director or managing editor takes care of hiring and supervising the checkers. A fact-checker may work on several articles at once, and those with less experience will more likely check shorter pieces while more seasoned checkers take on complex narratives or other substantial features. Each story typically has a writer and at least one main editor (other editors, often those who are higher up in the magazine hierarchy, may read the story as it is closer to its final state). Depending on the outlet, the fact-checker may interact only with the editor, only with the writer, or a little bit of both. The fact-checker receives the story after the writer and editor have gotten it to an agreeable near-final draft, which makes it easier to fact-check since the editing process usually deletes a swath of facts and creates new ones as sentences are removed, shifted, or added.

As a fact-checker, the actual process of double-checking source materials isn't your only important role. You'll have to do this while navigating your relationships with the writer and editor. Sometimes, these relationships will be smooth and supportive, but other times you will be suggesting changes that may make these folks bristle. How you deliver your message will make a big difference in whether your changes are ultimately accepted. This chapter also provides suggestions on how to handle yourself while working with your team.

FACT-CHECKING MAGAZINE ARTICLES

Step 1: Read

The first step, always, is to read the story you are checking. Your job is to familiarize yourself with it, but with a skeptical eye: no matter how great the writer or how seasoned the editor, don't trust everything they've said. You may eventually undo some of their lovely prose, clunking up the sentences to make them more accurate. Prepare yourself.

After you've read the story once, and if you have time, which many checkers won't, try to find a few articles on the same topic from reliable publications—think the *New York Times* rather than an anonymous personal blog. Don't use these as sources or even guidance, but to see other angles and representations. Maybe your writer is taking a provocative stance, or maybe previous stories have been wrong or incomplete. Or maybe the piece you need to check makes assertions that go beyond what one can logically draw from the facts or is missing a vital perspective. Whatever the case, you should try to get a sense of where your story fits in the subject's broader ecosystem. In addition to checking the black-and-white facts, you'll need to at least ask the editor or writer about these gray areas.

Indeed, think about the facts that are there as well as the facts that are missing. Are there any holes in the story? Is it inaccurate not because of the facts that are there, but because of what's been left out?

"To say that we're just checking facts—like the spelling of names or people's ages—isn't quite right," says Michelle Ciarrocca, a fact-checking veteran at *Vanity Fair*. "We are really digging in, reading the backstory, reading the context, and making sure that the tone is right and the sources are getting a fair shake."

Step 2: Identify the Sources

Contact the writer (or the editor, if you don't have a direct line to the writer) early on and ask for the source materials for the story, which may include notes, transcripts, interview recordings, reports, books, and contact information for key sources. Ask—delicately—if there are any parts of the story that either the writer or editor is worried about, or sources that are difficult to work with, which might help you identify sections that need extra attention.

The fact-checker's dream writer will also provide an annotated copy of the story. This means that within the electronic document—whether it exists in Microsoft Word, Google Drive, or another word-processing software—specific words, sentences, or even entire paragraphs will have comments, footnotes, or endnotes listing the relevant sources.

This won't always happen. Some writers will send a list of contacts and a folder of audio files, none of which have been transcribed. Some will send links to Wikipedia and unverified blog posts. Others will send nothing at all and will conveniently take off on a reporting trip, only to be reached in case of emergency via satellite phone at odd hours of the day during which they will be grumpy. Whatever the case, if you don't have the backup you need, talk to your editor and sort out a way to get better source lists from the writer. If this doesn't work, you may have to find your own sources (see chapter 4 for sourcing tips).

Step 3: Mark the Facts

Print a copy of the story—double-spaced with extra-wide margins is best, to leave room for notes. Arm yourself with your writing tools of choice and read the story again, marking each word or phrase that contains a fact. And yes, this may mean that you'll mark the entire document (if you didn't underline nearly every word in the previous chapter as part of the "Think Like a Fact-Checker" exercise there, go back and rethink your approach). Minimalists may prefer a single shade of pen or highlighter, while the sort of people who daydream about spreadsheets or enjoy diagramming sentences may use a system that is far more complex, with a different color for each type of fact—say, pink for quotes, yellow for proper nouns, green for the subjective murkiness that may creep into a writer's claims. Others prefer to use a different color per source.

The longer the story, the greater the need for a good fact-tracking system, says David Zweig, a former checker at *Vogue* and the former research head at the now-defunct *Radar*. For long features, Zweig recalls color-coding not only types of

North America's cricket industry didn't spring from a spontaneous, collective epiphany about shifting food tastes. Rather, it can be traced to two catalysts. The first was a 2010 TED talk by Dutch ecological entomologist Marcel Dicke that has been viewed 1.2 million times. Clicking through a Powerpoint in a beetle-adorned T-shirt, Dicke lays out the case for eating insects. A burgeoning population will not only add more mouths to feed, he points out, but will require increasingly more protein. The Food and Agriculture Organization (FAO) of the United Nations estimates that a population gain of 30 percent will require 70 percent more food; as people grow richer they want more meat, which requires more grain for feed. Then there's the economic argument. "If you take 10 kilograms of feed you can get one kilogram of beef," says Dicke. "But you can get nine kilograms of locust meat. If you were an entrepreneur, what would you do?"

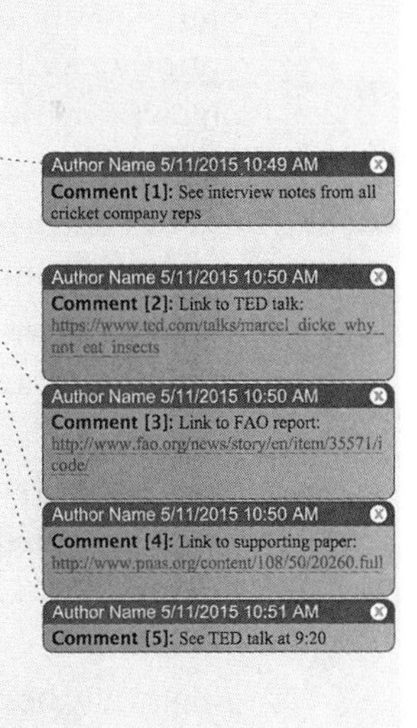

Author Name 5/11/2015 10:49 AM
Comment [1]: See interview notes from all cricket company reps
Author Name 5/11/2015 10:50 AM
Comment [2]: Link to TED talk: https://www.ted.com/talks/marcel_dicke_why_not_eat_insects
Author Name 5/11/2015 10:50 AM
Comment [3]: Link to FAO report: http://www.fao.org/news/story/en/item/35571/icode/
Author Name 5/11/2015 10:50 AM
Comment [4]: Link to supporting paper: http://www.pnas.org/content/108/50/20260.full
Author Name 5/11/2015 10:51 AM
Comment [5]: See TED talk at 9:20

Figure 4. One way a writer may annotate a story is with comments. Each sentence or group of sentences should be highlighted with a comment, and the source information should be written clearly in that comment.

North America's cricket industry didn't spring from a spontaneous, collective epiphany about shifting food tastes. Rather, it can be traced to two catalysts.[1] The first was a 2010 TED talk by Dutch ecological entomologist Marcel Dicke that has been viewed 1.2 million times. Clicking through a Powerpoint in a beetle-adorned T-shirt, Dicke lays out the case for eating insects. A burgeoning population will not only add more mouths to feed, he points out, but will require increasingly more protein.[2] The Food and Agriculture Organization (FAO) of the United Nations estimates that a population gain of 30 percent will require 70 percent more food;[3] as people grow richer they want more meat, which requires more grain for feed.[4] Then there's the economic argument. "If you take 10 kilograms of feed you can get one kilogram of beef," says Dicke. "But you can get nine kilograms of locust meat. If you were an entrepreneur, what would you do?" [5]

[1] See interview notes from all cricket company reps

[2] Link to TED talk:
https://www.ted.com/talks/marcel_dicke_why_not_eat_insects

[3] Link to FAO report:
http://www.fao.org/news/story/en/item/35571/icode/

[4] Link to supporting paper:
http://www.pnas.org/content/108/50/20260.full

[5] See TED talk at 9:20

Figure 5. Writers may also choose to annotate with either footnotes or endnotes.

information and the source where he found it, but using a number system to link a specific fact to its source—perhaps by writing the number next to the fact in the story as well as on top of a printed copy of the source.

In other words, there are many ways to organize our fact-checking, and none are necessarily right or wrong. Whatever system works for you is the best one, as long as it is thorough, consistent, and helps you track all of the information.

Step 4: Triage the Facts

What you do next depends on the story and how much time you have—some facts will be as wriggly as a freshwater eel, impossible to hold in your bare hands, while others will seemingly only be cleared from the mouth of a wise man meditating in a secluded mountaintop shack with no Wi-Fi. This is especially true when you have to speak with actual living, breathing people, each with their own schedules and priorities, to verify facts. Talking to you might not be a priority at all, as they may have already spent hours going through interviews with the writer or handing over documents and other materials. Contact these sources early—before you start fact-checking other sections that can be accomplished by reading printed or otherwise recorded source material, which you can work on in between source interviews—to make sure you can get through in time for your deadline. It may be helpful to collect all of the sources' contact information in one place, whether it's a Post-it note or a document saved on your desktop for easy access later on.

Not everyone likes a cold call, so when possible, use e-mail to set up a time to talk unless otherwise directed (you may also need to track people down through text messages, social media, and any other way you can find). If you are dealing with a person you think will be hard to reach—a celebrity, CEO, or university department head, for example—find the e-mail address for their publicist, assistant, or press department and include it on the message. Explain who you are, why you are writing, and how long you'll need to speak with the source. Also include your deadline.

While you're waiting to hear back from these sources, make a list of questions for each one so that you're ready for the interview. How you structure the questions will depend on the source and the type of story. If the source is, say, a scientist or technology expert, you may want to pull some of the same language from the story into the questions to make sure it's precise—words that pop up in science may have completely different meanings than in everyday use. On the other hand, if there is sensitive language that may cause the source to balk if they hear it out loud, try asking as many neutral questions as you can to prompt them to talk about the same topic.

Pay attention to how you word your questions. Although a simple yes-or-no format will work in some cases, sources may slide through these and answer incorrectly. Rather than spelling their name and asking if it is correct, word the question so that they have to spell it. Rather than offering a date and

Pro Tip: How to Contact Sources

When you e-mail a source, be polite, brief, and specific. You may want to say your deadline is earlier than it actually is, to allow for the occasional and unavoidable rescheduling. Here's a sample e-mail:

From: Vicky Verity <factchecker@magazine.com>
To: Professor Fancy-Pants <prof@universityx.edu>
Cc: University X Media <media@universityx.edu>
Subject: Important Magazine fact-check re: campaign donations (time-sensitive)

Professor Fancy-Pants,

I am a fact-checker at *Important Magazine*, and I am checking Jane Press's story on the legal implications for campaign donations. Ms. Press interviewed you for the piece, and I'd like to go over information that came from your conversations to confirm a few details. Do you have time for a brief phone call? I expect it will last around 20 minutes, and I need to speak to you by next Friday in order to meet our printing deadline. If you don't have time for a call, please confirm that you'll be able to answer the questions by e-mail.

Thanks very much,
Vicky Verity

asking if it's right, ask them for the date. Of course, the more complicated the question or concept, the harder it will be to avoid a yes-or-no question. Try to think of follow-up questions to double-check that the source is paying attention.

Once the questions are ready, go back to the story and work through the facts that don't require an interview. Some checkers do this line by line, while others—usually the ardent

Quick Guide: Triage Your Facts

Some facts will be more difficult to confirm than others. As you're reading through an assigned story, note which facts you think will be more difficult to find—such as those coming from a specific person, who may be traveling or otherwise hard to reach—as well as those that are easier, such as numbers from a study or dates when well-known events took place. Here's one way to organize your steps:

1. Contact each source ASAP to set up a phone interview.
2. Prepare the questions you'd like to ask each source (a separate document per source usually works best).
3. While you're waiting for sources to respond—or if you've already scheduled calls but have downtime to fill—check the easy facts that are based on documents or other tangible sources.

color-coders—clump the fact-check into specific categories of facts, or facts from the same type of source.

As you work through the story, you may find facts that aren't directly attributed to a person, but nonetheless would be easier to ask an expert than by deciphering reams of source materials—particularly if the concepts are complex. In this case, check the list of people who you're already planning to interview to see if any might be able to answer these questions. If so, add those questions to the list that you plan to work through once you get a chance to talk to those experts on the phone. For example, let's say the writer interviewed one of the sources about a new type of motor for an electric car, and you have a list of questions surrounding that. When you go through the story again, you might notice some other facts about general car technology that you don't have a good source for—if you add these to the question list for the electric car expert, even if they don't know the answers, they may be able to direct you to the right information or another person with relevant expertise. If you don't have an obvious expert on your list, find another on your own who can help (more on this in chapter 5).

For some sources, you will only have a few easy questions. To save time, you may want to simply include these in your original e-mail. But beware. A phone call may allow you to detect tone changes in the source's voice, which won't come across in an e-mail; these cues could lead you to dig further into a question and get more accurate details. It is also easier to ask follow-up questions, such as when a yes-or-no question is inevitable, but you want to double-check that the source is paying attention so you rephrase it and ask again. And in some cases, a phone call may uncover more information that e-mail will not. Take this example from *More*, provided by Beatrice Hogan. She once checked a story about Congresswoman Martha McSally, a former U.S. Air Force pilot who sued the Department of Defense in order to get rid of a rule that required women pilots to wear an abaya, a loose over-garment, when traveling off base in Saudi Arabia. The story's original structure indicated that the rule was overturned because of that lawsuit. In a phone call for the fact-check, McSally's chief of staff volunteered that the rule actually changed because Congress passed a law about it, a fact that Hogan says she would have missed if she had used basic questions laid out in an e-mail.

If you have a recorder, consider using it to keep an accurate record of your phone conversation with the source. Be sure to double-check the laws in your state: in some places, it's illegal to record someone without their consent. Even in places where it's legal, it's a better—and nicer—practice to simply tell the source you are recording the call to make sure you catch everything. If they object, explain that the recording isn't for broadcast, but for your notes and backup materials.

Quick Guide: E-mail vs. Phone Interviews

Fact-checkers are divided on which format is best for interviewing sources: e-mail or phone. E-mail provides a written and accessible record, and can be helpful for simple questions or for situations when a source can't be easily reached by phone. But phone interviews allow for follow-up questions and may tease out factual mistakes and nuance that are easily missed in an e-mail exchange.

Step 5: Track and Document

When a fact checks out, mark the relevant word or words—a check mark, an X, or a line through the word all work well—and write the source in the margin, right next to the sentence. Yes, it can get messy. If you have a lot of sources, you may want to make a numbered list in a separate document so that you only need to write the appropriate numbers in the margin.

If you need to make a correction, use common copyediting symbols to add suggested changes to the story. Most of these symbols, like a caret (^) to insert a word or letter or a ~~strike-through~~ for deletions, may be familiar from the essays your teacher marked up in high school. But there are three common marks that may be new. Two of these may appear in the original draft that you receive from the writer. One is "TK," and it is the fact-checker's enemy; the other is "CK," and it is neutral. The third new symbol is one that will appear throughout the fact-checking process: this is "stet," and although it can be frustrating, it may also be your friend.

The first two symbols usually work like this. When a writer doesn't have a fact to bolster a sentence, they may insert "TK" in its place. This is old printing shorthand for "to come" and it's supposed to suggest that the writer is still working to find the

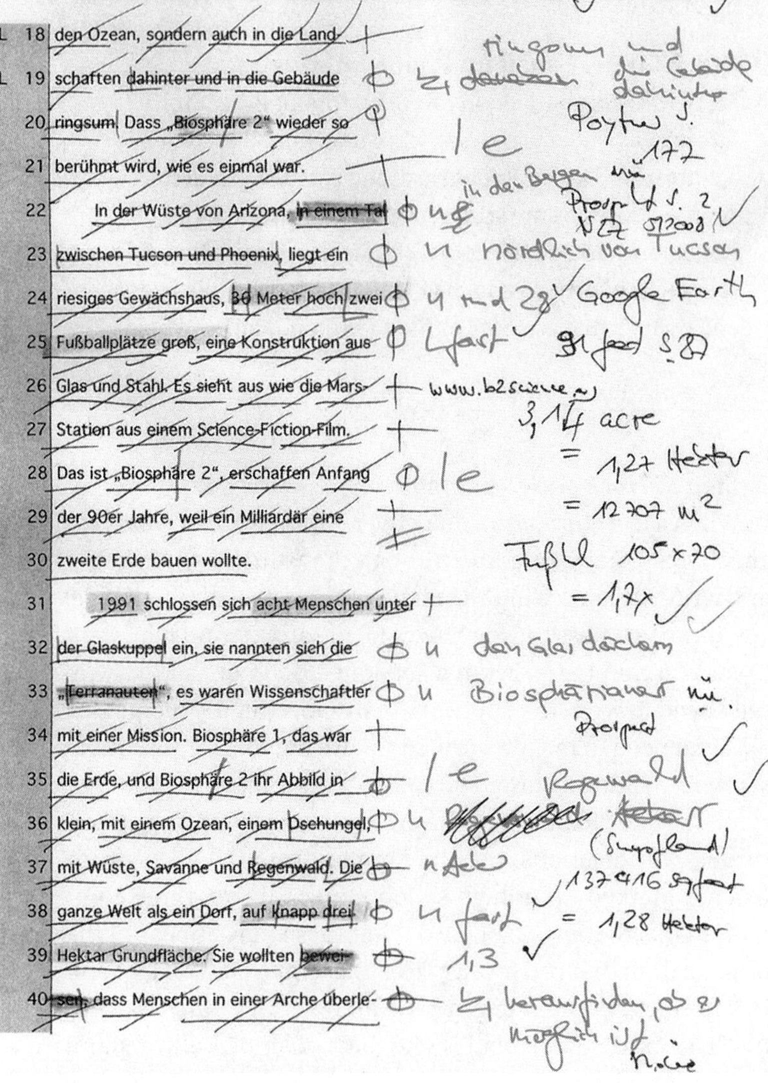
den Ozean, sondern auch in die Landschaften dahinter und in die Gebäude ringsum. Dass „Biosphäre 2“ wieder so berühmt wird, wie es einmal war.

In der Wüste von Arizona, in einem Tal zwischen Tucson und Phoenix, liegt ein riesiges Gewächshaus, 30 Meter hoch, zwei Fußballplätze groß, eine Konstruktion aus Glas und Stahl. Es sieht aus wie die Mars-Station aus einem Science-Fiction-Film. Das ist „Biosphäre 2“, erschaffen Anfang der 90er Jahre, weil ein Milliardär eine zweite Erde bauen wollte.

1991 schlossen sich acht Menschen unter der Glaskuppel ein, sie nannten sich die „Terranauten“, es waren Wissenschaftler mit einer Mission. Biosphäre 1, das war die Erde, und Biosphäre 2 ihr Abbild in klein, mit einem Ozean, einem Dschungel, mit Wüste, Savanne und Regenwald. Die ganze Welt als ein Dorf, auf knapp drei Hektar Grundfläche. Sie wollten beweisen, dass Menschen in einer Arche überle-

Figure 6. Fact-checker copies require systems of highlights and different colors of pens to track each fact and its source. Courtesy of *Der Spiegel.*

information. Since TK isn't an actual word or proper spelling, it provides a red flag to let printers, designers, and editors know that the text isn't final so that the letters don't accidentally appear in the final printed story.

TK may literally *mean* "to come" but some writers take a looser interpretation. Maybe the writer has given up; maybe they are lazy and decided to leave it for the fact-checker to fill in a statistic that supports whatever claim they've made. Either way, finding a good source will be up to you, but beware: the facts might not exist, so the sentence may simply need to be cut. Can't lie: this may give you pleasure.

Occasionally, you may see "CK." This isn't a misspelling of TK. Instead, it means "check." Of course, you should always check everything anyway. But CK, usually written in parentheses after the fact in question, means the writer is especially unsure of this specific fact or based it on memory with no identifiable backup source.

As for "stet," it is Latin for "let it stand," and it is used when an edit is made and then overturned. For example, you may find what you think is an error and offer a correction, but the editor may decide that you are being too picky and that the original text is better—the stet reverts the story back to that original text. The stet may occasionally frustrate you, particularly if it overturns a fact that you think is essential. But in order to get stets to work in your favor, keep track of who stets which facts in your story. If an editor or writer decides to ignore one of your factual changes, you should have a written record. You'll need this later if you were right and the story is printed with an error, because it's proof that you made the suggestion but it wasn't accepted.

When a fact is incorrect, explain why and offer the most elegant fix possible. Sometimes it's a matter of adding a qualifier or softening a claim. See the difference, for example, between "we will each have our own robot butler within the next decade" and "robot butlers may be common within the next decade." Keep your fix to roughly the same word count as the

Symbol	Definition	Example
^	Insert	Insert a or a missing ltter.
ℓ	Delete	Delete delete an extra or inaccurate word or letterr.
∾	Transpose	Swap the words order of or parts of a sentence.
/	Lowercase	Change a letter from Uppercase to lowercase.
≡	Uppercase	Capitalize a word, such as white house.
stet	Let it stand	Reverts an edited sentence back to its original.
TK	To come	The average story has TK of these.
CK	Check	The hippo is the largest land animal in Africa (CK)

Figure 7. Common copyediting symbols that may come in handy for a fact-checker.

original sentence. This is especially important for magazines—the number of pages and layout design limit how many words will fit. Of course, straightforward changes, such as dates or spelling, don't require an explanation.

Step 6: Report Your Findings

Once you've finished the first round of fact-checking, you'll need to tell the writer or editor what's wrong with the story. And there will always be *something* wrong, or at least portions that could be clearer or more tempered. Be diplomatic and kind. This is true even if the writer sourced the entire piece with Wikipedia and then took off on a phone-free Italian vacation the morning you started your fact-check. Diplomacy is important for three reasons. First, you might be wrong. The writer may have a better source that they forgot to send you, or new information may have unfolded in a breaking story. Second, even if you aren't working directly with a writer, you never know whether your words will make it back to them, and even the most seasoned or hardened writer might not take criticism well. Writers work hard on each story, maybe for months or even years, and you should respect that effort. And you may have to work together again. Third, and related, is that you have to convince both the writer and editor that your changes make the story better. If you start that process as a confrontation, it'll only make your job harder.

In order to share fact-check changes, most publications will require a fact-check report, although its format will depend both on you and your team. One common approach is to save the original electronic copy of the story as a new document. Use "track changes" to show each suggested edit as well as the information you've deleted. Include your source and any extra explanation in a comment, footnote, or endnote. Before you start changing things directly in the story, though, check with your editor: some may prefer that you keep the suggestions as footnotes or annotations, while others may want a list of corrections in a new document.

Separately, make a list prioritizing your changes that only you will see. Start the list with those that you feel are absolutely necessary—without them the story will be inaccurate or may even open the publication to a lawsuit. After you've written all of the must-haves, put the changes that fall into the gray area—that nebulous collection of words imbued with different meanings depending on who you are and how you are reading the story. The writer or editor may stet these, and that is fine so long as you raised the points. Put the smallest quibbles last—maybe the way the writer describes a style of music, for example, or the use of a common name rather than a formal one. Pick your list wisely, because in truth any sentence could be indefinitely tweaked for accuracy. There must be a compromise between your interpretation of the facts, the weight of those facts, and the reality of producing a compelling and readable story on deadline.

Step 7: Check Each Version

Fact-checkers who work at a print magazine will eventually see the story in layout, which is how it will look, more or less, in its final physical form, in which the magazine's art department stylizes it and includes graphics, photos, and special fonts. As a story works through final fact-checking and edits, it is usually printed on extra-large paper with wide margins, where you can write corrections and notes. These paper copies are usually called proofs. Magazines usually go through about three rounds of proofs per story. You should read each proof carefully to make sure your changes have made it from one round to the next. Also look closely for new text or other alterations. Editors love to sneak in sexy sentences to liven up a story, but they don't always source the changes. If this happens, ask the editor where these new facts came from, as well as for backup citations (tactfully point out that you need the information for record keeping). And finally, double-check the information that the art team has added to the headers and footers of the story, including the name of the magazine, the date it will publish, and the page numbers, as well as the information in the gutter (the middle seam where the pages will meet, which usually includes photo credit information and the like).

Some magazines publish on the Internet rather than in print, and for these publications, you won't see printed proofs. Still, fact-checkers at online outlets will also likely see a story before it goes live. As with a printed proof, read the draft carefully against your original fact-checking report to make sure your agreed-upon changes made it in; verify that the photographs and other images are correct; and look for new changes that the editor or writer introduced after the fact-check.

Think Like a Fact-Checker

Find a story from your favorite magazine or online publication, and identify all the facts, experimenting with whatever pen and highlighter combination is right for you if you're working on paper. *Bonus:* Look up each fact, and see if you can spot any mistakes. (Do not call or e-mail people who appear in the story; you will confuse them. Only check facts that don't require a conversation with a person.)

FACT-CHECKING OTHER MEDIA

Stories take many forms beyond a magazine or web article, of course. As such, there are unique considerations for checking other nonfiction media, including radio pieces, television segments, podcasts, and documentaries, as well as genres such as memoir or even poetry.

Audio and Video

Historically, neither radio nor video pieces have typically been extensively fact-checked—at least in the magazine sense, by a person who is not directly involved in producing the piece. But some narrative radio shows such as *This American Life*, *Serial*, and *Radiolab* have started using independent fact-checkers. A handful of outlets that produce videos have independent fact-check departments, too. One example is Retro Report, which makes short web documentaries that look at past media stories—some many decades old—and explores how they've held up over time. Another is the National Geographic Channel, which requires all in-house and contract producers to submit to a fact-check and even assesses the merit of show and series pitches before they are accepted. The quality of fact-checking across networks, however, is spotty—look no further than the Discovery Channel's controversial shows *Mermaids: The Body Found*, *Megalodon: The Monster Shark*, and *Eaten Alive* for examples where the fact-check was lacking. And as for daily news shows, while independent fact-checking isn't common because the quick turnaround makes the process difficult, some do work it into their daily routine. One example is *CBS Evening News with Scott Pelley*, which has a research and fact-check department that double-checks stories before they air.

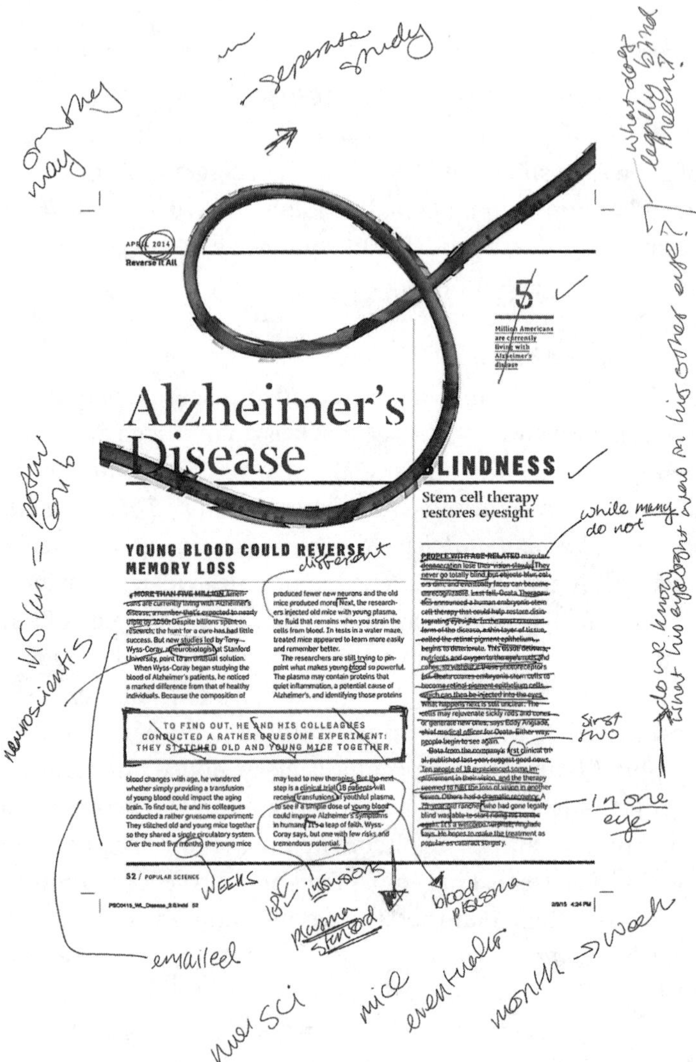

APRIL 2014
Reverse It All

5
Million Americans are currently living with Alzheimer's disease

Alzheimer's Disease

YOUNG BLOOD COULD REVERSE MEMORY LOSS

MORE THAN FIVE MILLION Americans are currently living with Alzheimer's disease, a number that's expected to nearly triple by 2050. Despite billions spent on research, the hunt for a cure has had little success. But new studies led by Tony Wyss-Coray, a neurobiologist at Stanford University, point to an unusual solution.

When Wyss-Coray began studying the blood of Alzheimer's patients, he noticed a marked difference from that of healthy individuals. Because the composition of blood changes with age, he wondered whether simply providing a transfusion of young blood could impact the aging brain. To find out, he and his colleagues conducted a rather gruesome experiment: They stitched old and young mice together so they shared a single circulatory system. Over the next five months, the young mice produced fewer new neurons and the old mice produced more. Next, the researchers injected old mice with young plasma, the fluid that remains when you strain the cells from blood. In tests in a water maze, treated mice appeared to learn more easily and remember better.

The researchers are still trying to pinpoint what makes young blood so powerful. The plasma may contain proteins that quiet inflammation, a potential cause of Alzheimer's, and identifying those proteins may lead to new therapies. But the next step is a clinical trial: 18 patients will receive transfusions of youthful plasma, to see if a simple dose of young blood could improve Alzheimer's symptoms in humans. It's a leap of faith, Wyss-Coray says, but one with few risks and tremendous potential.

TO FIND OUT, HE AND HIS COLLEAGUES CONDUCTED A RATHER GRUESOME EXPERIMENT: THEY STITCHED OLD AND YOUNG MICE TOGETHER.

BLINDNESS

Stem cell therapy restores eyesight

PEOPLE WITH AGE-RELATED macular degeneration lose their vision slowly. They never go totally blind, but objects blur, colors dim, and eventually faces can become unrecognizable. Last fall, Ocata Therapeutics announced a human embryonic-stem cell therapy that could help restore disintegrating eyesight. In the most common form of the disease, a thin layer of tissue, called the retinal pigment epithelium, begins to deteriorate. This tissue delivers nutrients and oxygen to the eye's rods and cones, so without it these photoreceptors die. Ocata coaxes embryonic stem cells to become retinal pigment epithelium cells, which can then be injected into the eyes. What happens next is still unclear. The cells may rejuvenate sickly rods and cones or generate new ones, says Eddy Anglade, chief medical officer for Ocata. Either way, people begin to see again.

Data from the company's first clinical trial, published last year, suggest good news. Ten people of 18 experienced some improvement in their vision, and the therapy seemed to halt the loss of vision in another seven. Others had a dramatic recovery. A 75-year-old rancher who had gone legally blind was able to start riding his horses again. It's a welcome surprise, Anglade says. He hopes to make the treatment as popular as cataract surgery.

52 / POPULAR SCIENCE

Figure 8. An example of a fact-checker's proof at a magazine. Courtesy of *Popular Science.*

Pro Tip: How to Adapt the Fact-Check Process Using Electronic Documents

Hate paper? Love trees? Or are you working remotely without a printer? A paper-based fact-check isn't always practical or preferable. The process listed for the basic magazine fact-check is still in play, but with significant changes to step 3 and step 5. Here's how to approach these steps:

MODIFIED STEP 3: MARK THE FACTS

Make a separate copy of the story file and rename it. Then, using your software tools, either highlight or boldface the entire text.

MODIFIED STEP 5: TRACK AND DOCUMENT

As you go through the story and confirm each fact, remove the highlight or bold text from the relevant words or sentences—this trick will both track the information you've already checked and provide a visual on how much more you need to do (go to "print preview" to see the whole story). List the source for each fact as a comment, footnote, or endnote.

If you need to fix an error, make sure to use "track changes" to show what has been deleted and what has been added. If appropriate, leave a brief and polite explanation for the change in the comment, footnote, or endnote, as well as the source information. When are you are finished, the document can serve as your fact-checking report.

Pro Tip: Checking Letters to the Editor

Even letters to the editor need to be fact-checked in magazines that print them. First, the fact-checker needs to confirm that the letter is authentic and that the person who signed it indeed wrote it. The letters are also usually edited for clarity, length, and house style, which will need to be relayed to the letter writer. Also check that the writer's name, title, location, and any other information are accurate. And finally, verify that the information in the letter is true—if it is an attempt to point out an inaccuracy or oversight in a story, make sure that there is indeed a mistake. If the story was correct and the letter is wrong, don't print the letter. Not only do you not want to print an inaccuracy, your media outlet is responsible for any potential defamatory claims in a letter.

In both radio and video pieces, the basic steps for fact-checking are similar to what you've already seen with a magazine or web story. The main differences are the documents you work with (scripts and audio or video cuts rather than articles), the people involved (producers and executive producers rather than writers and editors), and the time frame (often tight turnarounds versus a few weeks for a print story).

Both radio and video teams work from scripts. A fact-checker may receive a script early on, once a piece is close to its final form, or even after it is recorded and edited. Regardless, the producer for the piece should hand over source materials just like in a magazine fact-check, and the checker should follow the same steps. Scripts and edited cuts, however, are living documents that may change even within the hour before they air. Because of this, the fact-checker must work closely with the team and follow changes up to the point that the piece is live.

Videos have a visual dimension, too, which adds to the complexity of the fact-check. In addition to double-checking the accuracy of each image on its own, photographs and figures that appear on the screen during a television segment or documentary should accurately support what the news anchor or voice-over is saying. Also pay close attention to clips from other audio or video used to highlight an argument. Were the quotes or segments taken out of context? A checker should go back to the original source and listen to or watch the entire piece—or at least a good chunk of time before and after the quote appears—to make sure the clip is represented fairly.

And finally, when you're working with documentaries, keep in mind that even filmmakers don't agree on whether they're journalists, storytellers, or a mixture of both. This type of audio or video piece will be strikingly different from a straightforward news story, and fact-checking will require balancing the filmmaker's goals with reality. Take, for example, the popular 2015 HBO documentary *The Jinx*, the true crime story about New York real estate heir and alleged murderer Robert Durst. The documentary was eerily compelling, but after the finale aired—and after Durst was arrested, just one day earlier—critics began questioning the timeline it presented. Certain details, they said, may have been held in order to make the story more dramatic.

Think Like a Fact-Checker

Watch a nightly newscast, and pay attention to how the words that the anchor is saying link up to the graphic elements, including maps, photographs, boxes of text, and information that may run in a ticker at the bottom of the screen. Can you catch any moments where the graphics and verbal reportage don't align? If you had been fact-checking the piece, what changes would you have suggested?

Books

NONFICTION

It may surprise the average reader to learn that most publishers of nonfiction books don't do a formal fact-check. The publisher may have a lawyer look over the book to flag potentially libelous content, but beyond that, it is up to the author to make sure the book is accurate. And while there are hints this may be changing at some publishing houses, the responsibility for fact-checking will usually fall to the author.

Some authors approach fact-checking by ignoring the process entirely. Others hire an independent fact-checker, do the fact-check themselves as best as they can, or a combination of both. Usually, the latter two choices are a matter of financial constraints: book advances are often too modest to support the cost of a checker, which means the author must pay out of pocket. But let's say you land a great book-checking gig. A book manuscript may be 80,000 or 100,000 words or more, many times that of even the heftiest narrative magazine feature. How do you even begin?

Even before you start fact-checking, you should talk to the author about expectations, timing, and budgets, says Emily Krieger, a writer and researcher who has fact-checked popular science books including the critically acclaimed *Spillover: Animal Infections and the Next Human Pandemic* by David Quammen. Book fact-checking work will most likely be freelance, and it's better to sort out the hourly rate and estimated time frame before you start the work. This process will help to avoid sticker shock over your invoice and will also help you and the author identify which sections or types of facts need the most attention.

During the conversation, you should also ask what research materials you'll have access to, as well as whether the manuscript is footnoted or otherwise annotated (ask to see a sample chapter). If the manuscript has no annotations or you can't get your hands on the research material, your job will be much harder and take longer, which may become cost-prohibitive for the author.

If the job is agreeable and you move forward, the author should hand over their research materials and an annotated manuscript. You may get these relatively early on in the writing stage—maybe one chapter at a time—or as a full manuscript, and the amount of time you will have to work on it will depend entirely on the author's deadline with the publisher. However you get the pages, don't think of the project as fact-checking a sweeping book. Instead, break it into smaller chunks. Work one chapter at a time and follow the same fact-checking process that you would with a magazine article, with the caveat that you should only check the types of facts or sections of the book that the writer asked for (this may range from checking everything to focusing on lighter facts like numbers and spelling).

If you need to interview people who appear in the book—or experts who were interviewed but aren't specifically mentioned—and you don't have the full manuscript yet, ask the author whether these sources appear in multiple chapters. If so, you might want to wait until you've seen all of the relevant sections before making contact to set up a fact-checking interview.

As you work through the book, periodically check in with the author with updates on how much time you've spent, adjusting your price and timing estimates as needed. When you are finished, prepare a fact-checking report like you would with a magazine piece.

Think Like a Fact-Checker

The next time you read a nonfiction book, choose a page and underline each verifiable fact. Make a list of the sources you would use to check each fact. *Bonus:* Take the next step and fact-check the section (but again, don't contact any of the people who appear in the story). Did you find any errors?

MEMOIR

If nonfiction books don't usually go through a fact-check, then memoir is even further removed from the process. Memoir is autobiographical, a person's own account of their life based on their memory. This genre can slide into dicey territory from a fact-checking perspective. Our memories are faulty both because of our neurological limitations and because we see ourselves from an undeniably biased perspective.

Still, a wildly inaccurate memoir can get a writer or a publisher in trouble. Just ask James Frey, the author of *A Million Little Pieces,* which was published in 2003. Frey marketed the book as a true story about his drug addiction and rehabilitation. It was a best seller thanks, in part, to rave reviews by Oprah Winfrey. But a lengthy investigation by the website the Smoking Gun found that Frey fabricated much of the account, including his own alleged police records.

Your chances of getting hired to fact-check a memoir are probably slim. But if given the opportunity, you should start by asking about the publisher's goal. Do they want you to check straightforward facts, like names, dates, and timelines, to make sure they match the author's memory? Or do they need a more investigative take, like double-checking police reports and school graduation records, or speaking with friends or family members to see if their memory of an event aligns with the author's? Or are they worried about libel, which could result from a writer exposing inaccurate statements about their family and friends?

FICTION

Now we're in even slipperier territory: by definition, fiction doesn't claim to be factual. Look no further than the disclaimer at the beginning of a novel or movie, which usually says something like this: "The following work is fiction. Names, characters, places, and events are either a result of the author's imagination, and any resemblance to actual people, living or dead, or to situations or incidents is entirely coincidental." Still, a lot of great works of fiction are rooted in real worlds—or at least believable ones—and making sure certain details are correct can help bolster these backdrops.

While it's not typical for a piece of fiction to go through a formal fact-check, some book editors or copy editors may flag inaccuracies that don't support the world that the author is trying to build. Examples may include anachronism, such as referencing a technology that didn't exist at the time the story takes place. If this is a science fiction novel, then the reference may be intentional. If it is historical fiction, it may be an oversight. Or, perhaps, the author inadvertently put a real and famous landmark on the wrong side of a city, or misspelled the name of an actual political figure. Regardless, a good editor or copy editor will spot these inconsistencies to help make the fictional world as rich with accurate details as possible.

Reviews, Criticism, Columns, or Other Opinion Pieces

Reviews and criticism may cover anything from a book to a movie to an album to a play to an exhibit at a museum. Whatever the object of the review, the fact-checker should look into it—read the book, watch the movie, listen to the album, go to the play, visit the museum (or get on the phone with the curator, if it's in another city). The most important part will be checking to make sure the details that the reviewer references are accurate. The rest of the review will likely be opinion based on the reviewer's expertise—presumably, that's why the publication asked this specific person to write it. It's tough to fact-check these more subjective aspects, but if there are any assertions that ring entirely untrue based on what you have seen or watched or heard, bring up your concerns to the editor.

Columns are a bit like reviews in that they're soaked in opinion. The facts within them need to be right, but a checker won't have much control over the conclusions a columnist draws from these facts. Check what you can and give your editor a heads-up on opinions or claims that seem outlandish, particularly those that could draw legal action.

And in general, fact-checking the writer's opinion in a piece isn't necessary as long as the opinion is based on facts. If the writer makes a judgment about someone's physical appearance—for example, writing that a man has a scraggly black beard—you don't need to check with the man that his beard is scraggly. Confirm he has a beard, check a photograph if it is available, and move on.

Miscellaneous

The list of items that may be fact-checked is infinite—if a piece of writing exists, you can probably find *something* about it that can be double-checked. In addition to various news media or books, there is also poetry, advertising, cartoons, and more. For the most part, a fact-checker won't encounter these unusual cases, but in the rare times that you do, you can tailor the fact-checking process regardless of the format. Poetry, for example, may reference real-life events, and it's important to consider whether the author purposely twisted these to make a point or slipped up by accident. Advertising—especially for products that make claims related to health or medicine, as in the pharmaceutical industry—may require in-house checkers to pore over supporting studies. If a brand says their products are scientifically proven to smooth your wrinkles, they have to have evidence or risk the wrath of the Federal Trade Commission, which penalizes companies for false advertising.

As for cartoons, Carolyn Kormann at the *New Yorker* says to ask yourself: Do you understand the joke? Are spellings and meanings of words correct, particularly those in foreign languages? Do the representations of specific animals or individuals make sense—e.g., is Superman's "S" right? Do the descriptive details of a place match reality—e.g., does the North Pole inaccurately show penguins, which actually only live in the Southern

Hemisphere? Are all logos and mascots depicted correctly? And are sartorial details appropriate—e.g., the placement of the buttons on a men's versus a women's dress shirt?

In one example from the *New Yorker*, Kormann recalls a Harry Bliss cartoon that showed the "Here's Johnny" scene from *The Shining*, with Jack Nicholson's ax replaced with a fluffy white dandelion blowball. Shelley Duvall, who plays Nicholson's wife in the movie, holds a box of tissues instead of a knife, and the caption reads: "Here's Pollen." Trouble is, says Kormann, dandelion blowballs don't carry any pollen. Bliss redrew the image using a flowering dandelion instead.

Think Like a Fact-Checker

Pick whatever media you're consuming at the moment—whether it's a novel, a podcast, or a television documentary—and select a short section (maybe a page for a printed work or a minute for audio or video). As you read, listen, or watch, make a list of the facts. *Bonus:* Look up each fact and see if you can spot any mistakes. (Do not call or e-mail people who appear in the story. It will confuse them.)

NAVIGATING RELATIONSHIPS WITH EDITORS, WRITERS, AND PRODUCERS

Knowing the steps required to fact-check a story is only part of the job. In fact, even if you are an expert researcher and can do these steps in your sleep, you will get nowhere as a checker if you don't learn how to approach relationships with the people you need to work with—namely, editors, writers, and producers.

As with many relationships, diplomacy is key. No matter how wrong you think the writer and editor are for including a bad fact in a story, keeping calm will help you accomplish your job. And if they still don't cooperate with you, hey, you tried.

Just make sure to keep a good record—either paper, electronic, or both—of your interactions so you can point to them if the story ends up needing a correction.

Writers—or producers, if you're working with radio or video—will likely feel closer to the story than anyone else, and changes may be especially difficult for them. Approach these people respectfully. Let them know you liked the story (even if you didn't, try to find something positive to say). Rather than pointing mistakes flat out, tell them you found sources with conflicting information and ask if they have anything else that supports what the story says. "Sometimes fact-checkers want to find the flaws in the story, and that's what you're doing," says Mark McClusky, the head of operations at *Wired* and a former fact-checker at *Sports Illustrated*. "But the point is not to play 'gotcha' with award-winning writers—it's to make them look as good as possible."

If you do think there needs to be a change, have a solution at the ready. Talk through it with the writer if appropriate, but if you find that conflict is unavoidable, tell the editor or the executive producer, who is ultimately the one in charge.

Magazine or web editors want every story to be right, but they are also preoccupied with many stories that are publishing simultaneously as well as juggling early drafts for next month's magazine or tomorrow's web posts. For video or audio stories, executive producers will be similarly busy. Don't come to these people each time you hit a small problem; rather, work through as much of the piece as possible, make a list of outstanding issues, and schedule a time to go through them. And again, if you've found a problem, have a suggestion on how to fix it (keep in mind the new material will need to fit the same amount of space for a magazine or time for a video or radio piece). Caveat: If you run into a very big problem, like a key source refusing to cooperate or evidence of plagiarism, tell the editor or producer as soon as possible.

Think Like a Fact-Checker

The next time you find yourself poised to argue with a friend or family member over a point of fact—say, in a friendly debate over the health care system or what happened last night on *The Bachelor*—find a way to calmly and diplomatically present your evidence and see whether you can persuade them to change their mind. (Disclaimer: Research suggests it's incredibly hard to change people's minds even in the face of hard empirical evidence, but it's good practice for adjusting your tone and your tact in the workplace.)

FACT-CHECKING ON A BUDGET

There is no way around it: fact-checking is tedious. It takes time. It takes money. It takes resources. Depending on where you work, you may not be able to read the story multiple times, mark it up like a Day-Glo rainbow, and find primary sources for every fact. So, what should you do if you're asked to fact-check under these circumstances?

At the very least, you should look for potential legal liabilities and obvious errors. It's not the best approach, but it's better than nothing. Print a copy of the story, take a pen, and mark any points that might be contentious or controversial as well as all of the items that are most easily checked and easy to get wrong: proper nouns, unusual spellings, places, prices, dates, and so on (if you can't print, or don't want to, do the same by highlighting these sections or words on an electronic document).

The controversial bits hopefully will check out based on the writer's sources, but you still may need to talk to the editor to see if the publication should consult a lawyer. If you don't have access to a lawyer and you can't confirm the information based on what the writer has provided, here are a few suggestions: (1) ask that the story's publication be held while you track down appropriate confirmations, (2) soften the language so that it doesn't open the publication to a lawsuit, or (3) cut the most outrageous claims completely. If the editor doesn't agree with your take, you've done your due diligence in bringing it up. Just be sure to keep a written record as to who made the decision and when.

For the simpler facts, like spelling and prices, work your way through the fact-checking process laid out in the previous pages. You might have to rely on more online sources than actual people—say, for example, double-checking a price with a website instead of a publicist—but at the very least find the official online representation of a person or product to confirm information.

Think Like a Fact-Checker

Find a short blog post or news story and identify all the facts you would ideally check, but give yourself ten minutes to check the most important ones. Did you find any mistakes? If so, where do you think the author went wrong while sourcing the story?

FACT-CHECKING YOUR OWN WRITING

Many writers will never work with a fact-checker or research desk, particularly newspaper reporters, bloggers, and nonfiction book authors. If that's you, how can you apply the rigor of fact-checking to your own work?

It's not easy, and many checkers will even say it's impossible or bad practice. A fact-checker brings an outside eye to your stories, catching leaps of logic you may have taken in order to build an interesting piece. When it's just you, there is no way to step outside of your brain, which is rife with its own assumptions and blind spots.

Still, there are outlets that don't employ fact-checkers, and both time and money often limit hiring one independently. In cases like this, there are ways to distance yourself from your work in order to fact-check it as best as you can. For starters, always build time into your deadline so that you can step away from the story before it goes to your editor (or before it publishes, if you're blogging without an editor). Ideally, this will be days or even weeks. In reality, especially publishing on the web, this may only be an hour or two. Whatever your time frame, put the story aside for as long as you can and come back to it with fresh eyes. Try to look at it from the perspective of a skeptical fact-checker who doesn't necessarily trust your sources or claims, or an antagonistic reader looking for something to challenge. If you have time, print a copy out and follow the fact-checking process as though you were checking someone else's work. Make sure you keep your sources organized so that it is easy to go back to them (some writers annotate their stories as they work, dropping in footnotes with website links, source names, or report titles, while others use software such as Scrivener, which help organize and track research).

During the fact-check, also think about the sources you've used. Are they solid? Are there any facts that need extra backup—especially those that might be controversial or open you to a lawsuit? If so, consider finding another source to confirm the information.

Another way to fact-check the work is to run the entire story by an expert. This shouldn't be someone who is in the story. Instead, find a person who is knowledgeable on the topic and has no stake in how it turns out—this gets easier if you have a regular beat and have built a solid network of sources you trust. Having an outside source isn't the same as a fact-check and shouldn't replace it, but it will help identify potential holes in the story, as well as questionable claims.

For longer projects such as a book, try a combination of these approaches. Send sections of the book to appropriate experts, but also go through the entire manuscript sentence by

Quick Guide: Checking Your Own Writing

- Step away from the story for as long as you can to read it with fresh eyes.
- Print the story and read it away from your desk to get a different perspective.
- Read the story through the eyes of a skeptical reader or angry commenter. What mistakes would they catch?
- Fact-check starting at the last sentence and work backward, so you don't get caught up reading the story and thus missing the facts.

sentence and double-check it against your original sources. As you check, reconsider the quality of those sources.

Think Like a Fact-Checker

Pick a short article you've published or a section of a longer piece. Print it out and work through the fact-checking steps. Did you find any mistakes? How did it feel to double-check your own work? If you were to publish the story now, are there changes you would make?

FOUR ||| Checking Different Types of Facts

Now that you know the basic fact-checking process, how should you actually check each fact? There are tricks for checking different kinds—confirming a quote, for example, may require unique jujitsu that just isn't necessary when you're double-checking the spelling of a state capital or the price of an iPhone. Here are tips for checking the major categories of facts that you'll likely encounter in your work, organized from the most common and (generally) straightforward to the murky and troubling. As you read, consider how Peter Canby, the head of the checking department at the *New Yorker*, defines fact-checking: it is simply "elevated common sense."

BASIC FACTS

Every story you check will have elemental information including proper names, spelling, dates, and geographical locations. Always use a primary source for these when possible; if not, most checking departments suggest two or three high-quality secondary sources per fact (see chapter 5 for the distinction between primary and secondary).

When confirming spelling, draw a diagonal line through each letter of the word as you read through the source material and keep an eye out for accents and other symbols (see fig. 6). Double-check trademarked names, which may use unusual letters or capitalization (think Kleenex and BAND-AID). If there is a generic reference to the timing of an event ("last month"), make sure it will still be accurate whenever the story will publish. Similarly, always double-check a person's age with them, as they may have had a birthday—or will have one—between the time the story was written and when it goes to print (one former *Slate* intern recalls an awkward assignment where she had to call Martha Minow, a dean and professor at Harvard Law School, for the sole purpose of confirming Minow's age).

Read source material carefully to make sure you have the right person, place, or thing, and be wary of seemingly obvious facts that may have more than one meaning. Dan Sullivan and Dan Sullivan each ran for office in the Alaska Republican primaries in 2014, although they are two different men; Manhattan Beach is both a wealthy seaside community outside of Los Angeles and a tiny inland town in Minnesota; and if you're checking a story in Australia, you'll find that Americans have a very different meaning for a piece of clothing called a "thong."

Also beware of obsolete information online or in print. A university website may not reflect a recent change in a professor's title; a company may no longer offer a product at a certain price; and the phone number on a pamphlet for an Argentinian estancia, which a writer grabbed while working on a travel piece, may actually be out of service. When in doubt, call or e-mail a representative from whatever organizations are in the story to make sure the details are right.

Finally, don't assume that the writer and editor are using specific words correctly, particularly if those words are unfamiliar to you. When in doubt, check definitions to make sure the meaning and context are appropriate.

Think Like a Fact-Checker

The next time you read an article or a nonfiction book, pick one of the people mentioned in the story and—without actually contacting them or anyone else—try to confirm the details that were written about them. Were the sources hard to find? Did you notice discrepancies between the story and the information you found? If so, why might the writer have gotten it wrong—or why might the source you found be wrong?

NUMBERS

If you need to confirm numbers in a story, keep in mind the context, the source, and common sense. For straightforward measurements, this will be easier (but never slack even with these). Say, for example, you're fact-checking a feature in a food magazine that includes a recipe. Do the measurements make sense? Would anyone ever *really* use a tablespoon of vanilla extract, or is that meant to be a teaspoon? Or say you're fact-checking a story that cites distances that came from a report that was written in a European country. Were the measurements correctly converted from kilometers to miles? Or say a story claims that 8 billion people have purchased the latest smartphone. As of 2016, the world population was around 7 billion. Did the writer mean 8 million? Or how about a story on a new camera setup, which includes several attachments, that claims the entire kit can be purchased for $500. When you add up the individual prices for all the parts, does the price match up? Or how about a case where a writer rounds up or down, rather than using an exact number? It's usually best to use the exact number if it's available, but at the very least, let the writer and editor know the exact versus rounded numbers so they can make an informed decision on which to use.

The more complex the number, the more you need to pay attention. Take statistics, which are regularly twisted and misinterpreted. Look carefully at the sources that the writer used. Are the authors of those sources obviously biased in any way? Do they work for a partisan think tank, for example, or an advocacy group? If so, find a better, more neutral source, and make sure it is a primary one. (Unless the whole point of using that source is to point out its inherent biases, which should be made clear in the story.)

You also need to make sure the writer is using the stats correctly. A widely misunderstood example comes from health reporting, where studies often discuss *relative* risks but writers report them as *absolute* risks. Relative risk compares two different test groups, while absolute risk describes the actual likelihood of a specific event happening. Let's say a hypothetical study claims that jelly beans increase your relative risk of cancer by 25 percent. Inevitably you will see headlines saying "Jelly Beans Boost Cancer Risk by 25 Percent," which make it seem as though if you eat a jelly bean, you're in trouble. But now let's look at this hypothetical study more closely: the authors are comparing a group that eats jelly beans to one that does not. The non-jelly-bean-eaters had a 0.001 percent risk of cancer while the jellybean eaters had a 0.00125 percent risk. That's a 25 percent increase in relative risk, but it's still a tiny risk overall. Now, go eat a jelly bean.

Another example of misunderstood statistics comes from the inevitable headlines that follow announcements from the International Agency for Research on Cancer, which is part of the World Health Organization. The IARC is tasked with, among other things, looking at the available science on an array of materials and determining how likely it is that those materials cause cancer. The trouble is that the agency organizes these materials not by risk, but by the strength of the evidence. In 2015 their assessment of bacon made the news, with some outlets claim that it is just as likely to cause cancer as tobacco. In reality, while both tobacco and cured meats are included at the highest level on the IARC list ("Group 1: Carcinogenic to Humans") this only means that the science that confirms this connection is equally robust. In reality, eating bacon is far less risky than smoking when it comes to increasing your chance of cancer.

Yet another important statistical concept for a fact-checker to understand is the so-called p-value, which is how researchers try to determine whether the results from a study are statistically significant or due to random chance. A commonly

Pro Tip: Finding Numbers Online
Google isn't always a great source on its own, but it may help locate key numbers. If you can't confirm a statistic that appears in a story you are checking, try using search terms that include the number and other keywords from the sentence or sentences and Google may return a primary source. But beware: There may be even better sources that provide more accurate numbers, which likely won't come up in a search such as this. Evaluate whatever source Google spits out just as you would any other.

accepted p-value is 0.05, which translates to the researchers being 95 percent certain that their results represent something real. But in some areas of study, such as high-energy physics, a 0.05 p-level is laughably high. In other instances, researchers manipulate data until they reach an acceptable p-value—a process that is called p-hacking, which uses statistics improperly in order to squeeze out a desired answer. When in doubt, a fact-checker should call a statistician to help identify whether a paper is using the p-value honestly and correctly.

Finally, there may be cases where writers use raw data to make their own calculations. If possible, have the writer walk you through the math and take a look at the original sources used. Do those sources seem solid? Does the author's logic make sense? Can you find any other sources that help confirm the numbers?

If you're trying to check a stat or calculation and, despite having a solid source, the numbers still seem confusing, that's okay. You aren't required to be an ace statistician or math whiz to be a good fact-checker. Pick up the phone and call an appropriate expert, perhaps through the math department at an accredited university.

Think Like a Fact-Checker

The next time you read a magazine article, mark all the numbers. Can you track down reliable primary sources for each one? Which numbers proved the most difficult to check, and why do you think that is?

QUOTES

Ask three fact-checkers how to confirm a quote and you'll likely get three different answers. Checking quotes also varies depending on the publication, the sensitivity of the quote, the source materials available, and the context. Here are a few ways to do it. Each has benefits. Each has pitfalls.

Audio Recordings

No checker has time to listen to many hours' worth of interview files—assuming the writer recorded an interview in the first place—but sometimes a writer will provide you with both the relevant file as well as the time stamp at which the quote occurs. But even exact words on a recording could be misleading: the quality may be poor or the quote may be taken out of context. If the recording is garbled, double-check the quote's content with the source (see below for tips). For context, take care to listen to the audio both before and after the quote to make sure the way it is used in the story reflects what the person actually meant.

Transcripts

It's helpful to check quotes with a transcript if you're pressed for time, because you can run a search for a word or a phrase in the quote. But the quality of a transcript depends on how carefully a writer or a transcription service has followed a recorded interview, again assuming the interview was even transcribed. Maybe they misunderstood a phrase or mistyped a word. One cautionary tale comes from *Wired*. In 2013 the magazine published a story about Dropbox, a company that provides cloud storage so that a person can access their files from any computer. Marcus Wohlsen, the author of the story, quoted the company's co-founder Drew Houston this way: "You think about who needs Dropbox, and it's just about anybody with nipples." Wohlsen heard this version of the quote when he transcribed the interview, and the fact-checker confirmed the quote against that transcript. But after the story published, the magazine had to make a correction: Houston hadn't said "anybody with nipples" but "anybody with a pulse."

Check with the Source

Most publications forbid reading a quote back to sources verbatim—the source may deny it, or want to tweak it so they sound better or smarter or to avoid getting in trouble with, say, their employer. But if you don't have a reliable audio file or transcript, or if the writer handed you a quote scribbled on napkin or claimed to have pulled the quote from memory, you may need to check it with the source.

There are a few ways to do this, and which one you choose will depend on your employer's rules as well as whether the quote is benign or contentious. One option is to ask the source several questions on the same topic to see if you can catch something like the original quote. If their answer is similar to the original quote, it's reasonable to believe that the original quote is legit, although pay attention not only to the words they use but also their tone (are they saying it sarcastically, when the text comes off as earnest, for example?). Another method is to paraphrase the quote and ask if the information within it is true without disclosing that it is a direct quote in the story. Another is to tell the source you are paraphrasing a direct quote to make sure the information within it is accurate, although be sure to explain you can't make changes that don't deal directly with facts (some fact-checkers say this and then read the quote verbatim, especially if there is technical language within it). And even though it's not common, some publications do read the quote verbatim—and tell the source so—with the understanding that the magazine has the final say on whether to make any changes.

What should you do if the quote doesn't check out? Point it out to the editor in your fact-check report. At some publications, altering a quote in any way is forbidden; at others, deleting *ums* and *ers* and smoothing grammatical errors is okay; others, particularly those who write about technical issues for a general audience, may swap out a bit of jargon for a more digestible word, so long as the source agrees; and others rewrite quotes entirely to make the text snappy (not recommended!). Also be aware that most outlets edit long Q&A's for clarity and length, which means these will rarely exactly reflect the original interview. Usually, though, the writer will note that the Q&A has been edited in the piece's introduction.

There is also the matter of checking facts within a quote. If a source says something that is outside of their expertise or obvious knowledge, you'll need to check that claim. For example, if an artist references an anecdote about Picasso, who the artist obviously never met because their lives didn't overlap, find another expert or historical document to make sure that the story is accurate. If it isn't, the quote may not support the piece the way the author intended and it may need to be cut or replaced.

Think Like a Fact-Checker

Find a family member or friend who will let you record a short mock interview with them, or watch a video that you can record or otherwise play back. Take notes on what you hear. Later, try to reconstruct a quote with your notes, and then listen to the recording to see if you got it right. Was it difficult or easy to capture the quote correctly? Why might it have turned out that way—was the person a fast talker, or were they speaking about an unfamiliar topic, or was there a lot of background noise?

CONCEPTS

Some facts aren't discrete numbers or bits of information; instead, they are sweeping explanations about complicated concepts. Consider, for example, the leading theory of dark matter—the invisible material that may make up the bulk of the mass in our universe—or a political philosophy examining the rise of ISIS, or a sketch of the influences on Baroque music in the 1600s.

You will be a floundering novice to a lot of the subjects you must fact-check; big concepts or descriptions may require the help of an expert rather than cramming a PhD's worth of background reading into a workday. There are two key approaches for finding the right expert. First, look at the list of interviewees from the story—you are likely already speaking to these people to confirm more specific information. Add a few general questions to the questions you plan to ask them.

Second, look for someone who doesn't appear in the story but is willing to chat about background information. Google will help: search for professors of cosmology to find a dark matter expert, for example, or look for academics who have written on ISIS or the history of the Baroque movement. If you can't find a specific person, search for universities or professional organizations with good reputations in whatever field you need to ask about.

What constitutes "good" will be up to your judgment. Look for accreditations where necessary, and be aware that groups with impressive names may still be considered fringe. Always double-check whether an organization is generally respected by experts in whatever field it is supposed to represent.

Once you've found a solid group, e-mail or call the relevant media or press department, explain what you are looking for, and ask for expert recommendations.

Think Like a Fact-Checker

The next time you read an article or a book, look for explanations on how a technical process works, or the inner functions of an obscure government agency, or a description of a political movement, or any other potentially complicated concept. If you were fact-checking that story, what experts or organizations might you turn to in order to confirm the information?

ANALOGIES

Writers use metaphor, simile, and other rhetorical tricks to capture complex concepts in a relatable way. But are those analogies accurate? Is it reasonable to call the world a stage or say the universe began with a big bang, or did the writer bite off more than they could hang their hat on?

Sometimes you can confirm an analogy using your own common sense. Take the example from chapter 3 that called certain facts as wriggly as a freshwater eel, impossible to hold in your bare hands. Are freshwater eels truly wriggly? And are they actually difficult to hold? A fact-checker might peruse YouTube videos of people catching eels in their hands, call an expert freshwater eeler, or use their own experience for straightforward analogies. Other times, though, an analogy may be used to describe a complex scientific process or an artistic movement or something else that is more esoteric. In these cases, take a look at your source list and work the wording into your list of questions. You may find that the expert strongly disagrees that the analogy is a good one and instead recommends an even better replacement.

Think Like a Fact-Checker

Consider the analogy that facts are as wriggly as a freshwater eel, impossible to hold in your bare hands, and confirm whether or not it is an accurate one. Are freshwater eels, indeed, wriggly and hard to hold in one's bare hands? Was this a good analogy in this section's context? Why or why not? Can you think of a better one?

IMAGES

Stories are usually accompanied by images, which provide key visual context. You need to confirm that all images in a story show what they claim to show.

Photographs

Make sure the subject is the right person, place, or thing. Some of this information may come from a publication's art department, a wire service, or directly from a photographer, but it doesn't hurt to confirm with other sources if you have time—try official websites, press contacts, and cross-reference with other stock photography sites. Anyone with personal knowledge of the photograph and its content is always best, but beware of sending a photo directly to one of your sources. In some cases, this may be fine—for example, if you need the world's foremost expert on cane toads to confirm that a photograph indeed depicts a cane toad. But if the image came from an in-house photo shoot, the publication may prefer not to send it out, to protect their work from leaking. And a person who appears in a story may try to talk you out of using a specific photo of them if they think it is unflattering.

Also make sure that the image is oriented correctly. In a more abstract image, perhaps of an unfamiliar animal, has the top been inadvertently switched to the bottom? Has an image accidentally been rotated so that the left is now at the right—perhaps lettering on a sign will provide a clue?

Captions need fact-checking, too. Are names, locations, and other features identified and spelled correctly? Does the information accurately describe what is in the photo? A fact-checker at a fashion magazine may need to confirm the material of a piece of clothing—whether that vest is leather or pleather, or that rose-print dress actually shows a different type of flower—as well as the style and designer, while someone working with a photography publication may need to double check a featured camera's make and model. Also look out for vague descriptions that need more context: a photograph that is simply captioned "City Hall," for example, may need clarification. City Hall in London will look very different from City Hall in New York or Topeka, Kansas.

Illustrations and Animations

A piece of art is always subjective, but it should be grounded in reality for a nonfiction story. If a drawing, graphic, or animation is supposed to represent an actual person, animal, building, body of water, book, movie, machine, tree, piece of candy, or anything really, then you should check it against the real-world version of that anything. In a drawing of poison ivy, make sure there are clusters of three leaves, not four; in a portrait of a celebrity, make sure their hair isn't shaded blond if it is actually black; and in an animation that shows the mechanism that drives the world's fastest roller coaster, make sure the depiction does not defy the laws of physics.

Infographics

These are only as good as the data on which they were built, so a first step is to make sure the source is reliable and complete. Check all numbers against the original data, and also make sure that visual representations make logical sense. The sections of a pie chart should not add up to more than 100 percent. A set of shapes that are supposed to depict relative sizes—say, circles representing several county populations—should actually physically depict those size differences, so get out the ruler and measure them. A graphical categorization of beer flavor profiles should not attribute a vanilla flavor to Centennial Hops.

Maps

Borders in parts of the world are constantly changing, particularly as nations split up or annex one another. As of 2015 there were between 189 and 196 countries worldwide, depending on which resource you trust. Even well-established lines are accidentally changed by major news sources: in on-air graphics, CNN once moved London 120 miles to the northeast, NBC allowed Vermont to swallow New Hampshire, and Fox replaced Iraq with Egypt. Always double-check maps with atlases, guides, and even Google Maps to confirm location, spelling, borders, and more. Other features to check: city names and locations, geographical markers such as major rivers or mountain ranges, and map keys or legends that describe distances or other information. Also pay attention to cardinal directions. Are north, east, south, and west in the appropriate locations? Are you sure? Some older maps may show south at the top of the page, and north at the bottom. Make sure you consider the context.

Credits

Finally, make sure that all images are credited to the appropriate person—the photographer, artist, almanac, and so forth. If you want to double-check that an image belongs to a specific person, see if they have an online portfolio and check whether the image is there, or if the work that you find seems reasonably similar in style to the image you are using (artist information should also be available through a publication's art department).

Think Like a Fact-Checker

Think about a topic that you know a lot about—let's use baseball as an example. Go to Google Images and search for "baseball infographics." Do these representations seem accurate to you? If anything seems off, what do you think should have been changed in order to make it accurate?

PHYSICAL DESCRIPTIONS

Not every story will be packed with physical descriptions, but longer narrative pieces will always have the likes of a dusty intersection or the smell of fresh grass or a kid with warm brown eyes. Or perhaps a story will explain the inner workings of a machine and, in doing so, sketch its gleaming surface or whirring hums.

In the best scenario, the writer will provide photos and detailed notes that they took while reporting the story, or at least provide visual references that they found online. But if not, there are other ways to make sure a scene is accurate. To confirm places, look for photographs and maps online, especially from official sources like a city website. Google Street View may help with specific buildings or intersections, although colors and other details may have changed. You might also confirm descriptions with the people who were interviewed for the story, if they were in the same place, or from a local library. For machines, products, or other objects, look for product web pages and track down a press contact. For people, look for official websites or online bios, or double-check photography that will be published along with the story. You could also ask a source directly. (Once I had to ask a pest control expert whether he indeed had a mustache in 1999.)

Think Like a Fact-Checker

The next time you read a description of a place in an article or a book, look up that place and see if it was depicted correctly. How would *you* have described it? *Bonus:* Find a description of your hometown, or any other place you're very familiar with, in an article online. Does the description contradict how you see this location? If so, why do you think the writer saw it differently?

SPORTS

Don't rely on written accounts of a game or a match when you're fact-checking a sports piece. Instead, see if you can find a video of the game online. Watch it to make sure the scores, descriptions, timing, and so forth match up to the writer's interpretation.

Think Like a Fact-Checker

Read David Foster Wallace's "Federer as Religious Experience," published in the *New York Times* on August 20, 2006. Now see if you can find one of the Roger Federer matches that Wallace describes. When you watch the match, do you see what Wallace saw? Do the basic facts—like scores or movements—check out?

HISTORICAL QUOTES AND STORIES

There are snippets of history that twist over time. Maybe a translator confused a word or phrase years ago, or someone inverted a number or letter. Or maybe someone attributed a quote to the wrong person or changed its wording, and the new version carried on indefinitely because it just sounded better that way. The best approach to find out for sure is to dig up the primary source, whether it's a first edition book or a set of letters. It's not always possible during a tight deadline, of course, but if you do have time, a story from Alice Jones, the director of research at *National Geographic Magazine*, highlights the great lengths that checking such facts may require.

In 2011 Jones was checking a story about the development of the teenage brain. The story included a Shakespeare quote from *The Winter's Tale*, which, according to the author, read: "there were no age between sixteen and three-and-twenty, or that youth would sleep out the rest; for there is nothing in the between but getting wenches with child, wronging the ancientry, stealing, fighting." But the more Jones looked, the more unsure she was of the exact quote. After looking through sources including *Encyclopaedia Britannica*, dictionaries, and quotation books, Jones found some versions that said "ten and three-and-twenty" instead of "sixteen and three-and-twenty."

Ultimately she contacted the Folger Shakespeare Library in Washington, DC, and a historian there looked up the original folio, which confirmed "ten and three-and-twenty." At some point, perhaps in the eighteenth or nineteenth century, someone changed the line and it had been written incorrectly ever since. (The quote ultimately stayed in the *National Geographic* story as "ten and three-and-twenty.")

There are ways around these impressive fact-checking acrobatics, particularly if you're in a time crunch. You can recommend removing the quote entirely, or adding that it is *often* cited this way or *usually* attributed to this or that person rather than claiming it outright as fact. This is not ideal. Sometimes, it is necessary.

Think Like a Fact-Checker

Try to confirm the following historical quotes. If you are uncertain whether online resources are pointing you in the right direction, identify a library or other organization that has original editions, letters, or other primary sources. (Do not actually call the library or organization; they will be confused if everyone who reads this book does so.)

"Well-behaved women rarely make history."
—Marilyn Monroe

"The only sure things in life are death and taxes."
—Benjamin Franklin

"God does not play dice."
— Albert Einstein

PRODUCT CLAIMS

Any company selling a product advertises it in a flattering way, even when the product doesn't work very well. When a journalist writes about a product, sometimes they take the company's words at face value. To make checking these claims stickier, most companies are protective of data that might support their claims, including proprietary formulas, designs, or studies. So what is a checker to do?

One option is to make sure that any claims in a story are attributed to the company or a spokesperson and not the author—this at least makes it clear where the information came from. Another option is to interview experts to see if the claims that the company makes are even possible (for example, talk to a dermatologist and a biologist who studies skin to gauge the effectiveness of a wrinkle cream, but make sure they don't have financial ties to the company or product). Some magazines test products, too, but keep in mind that this is subjective—a positive result might be due to the placebo effect, that wily psychological trick that makes a product seem to work by sheer force of wishful thinking.

If a product makes a particularly outrageous claim—one that could potentially harm a reader if they were to try it, or open the publication to a lawsuit—question whether the

Quick Guide: Elusive Facts

If you can't confirm a fact, or if confirming it will take more time than your deadline allows, evaluate how necessary it is for the story. If it isn't crucial, consider suggesting to the writer or editor that they delete it entirely. If your team balks, add words to make the sentence more accurate. Rather than stating questionable historical anecdotes as fact, for example, perhaps add the words: "According to lore . . ." or "Legend says . . ." or something similar.

As for historical anecdotes, the same holds true: use a primary source when possible. If you can't find one—or if it doesn't exist—think of ways to present the stories that don't claim that they are factual. If using the anecdote no longer makes sense in light of these hedges, consider cutting it.

story should include it at all. This is especially important for products related to health, like weight-loss pills, diets, or exercise plans. Or if it must be included, make sure the story has context that appropriately questions the product's validity.

Think Like a Fact-Checker

Watch an infomercial on television or online and write down all the claims that you'd want to double-check before including them in a story. Next to each claim, make a list of the types of experts or resources you would use to confirm or refute it.

FOREIGN LANGUAGES

Some research departments purposefully hire fact-checkers who speak foreign languages—the *New Yorker*, for example, has had checkers fluent not only in Spanish and French, but also Arabic, German, Hebrew, Mandarin, Portuguese, Russian, and Urdu. Not every publication has the resources for such a wide linguistic spread, though. So how do you fact-check information, phrases, and so on that appear in a language other than your own?

First, find out whether any of the writer's sources speak the language, or whether they employed a translator during certain interviews. If the information is straightforward, you may be able to check it during a quick interview with either or both people.

But if there are no appropriate sources or translators—or if the information is sensitive and twisting it might benefit those same people in some way—find a third party who can help dig into the words' true meanings. E-mail a university language department or a specific professor with expertise, or check with a translation service.

Keep in mind that some languages may have unique regional characteristics. In 2012 the Associated Press created a Spanish-language style book, *Manual de Estilo*, to help journalists in the Americas use universally understood words since there are so many differences from one locale to the next.* While universal terms might be best for certain stories, like an international news article, regional dialects and phrases might be more appropriate for others, like a narrative travel piece about a small town. Consider, for example, the following sentence, written in Spanish: *Voy a tomar la guagua para el mercado*. If you look up the phrase in the Dominican Republic

* NPR's *On the Media* did a related episode on July 4, 2014, and it is available online at http://www.onthemedia.org/story/spanish-ap-style-guide/.

Spanish and then look it up in the version spoken in Chile, you will find very different meanings.

FOREIGN OUTLETS

Fact-checking isn't uniformly common worldwide or even within any country. As such, you likely won't have much opportunity to work as a fact-checker overseas. However, it's important to consider these differences when you're reading foreign publications, particularly if you are working with a writer who is quoting or otherwise sourcing from them. If this happens, take a moment to research the publication and the location where it is published and consider whether it seems trustworthy.

Newspapers and magazines operating in countries with censorship laws or state-run media are another issue. Salar Abdoh, an Iranian writer, recalls working on a story in which a man and a woman met in an American bar. Abdoh knew he couldn't get that past his country's censors, so he changed it to a café in his piece. "As a writer, these are simple things, but even these can make you question your role," he says. And while it may be a simple thing, it's important to keep in mind that details both small and large may be altered—if a bar must be a café, what other ways may the truth be changed?

"COMMON KNOWLEDGE"

When a fact-checker asks for a source, one of the most irritating responses a writer can give is "Well, that's just common knowledge." By now, from reading this book, you know that even the simplest claims need to be double-checked. As the old journalism adage goes: If your mother says she loves you, get a second source. (Try to find the primary source on that chestnut.) No matter how obvious a fact or statement may seem, use your checker skills to check it out. For example, consider this piece of common knowledge: Washington, DC, is the capital of the United States. Think about how it is that you know this is true. Likely, you've read or heard this hundreds of times—so many that it'd feel silly to spend time looking it up in a primary source during a hypothetical fact-check. But now consider working on a story that mentions the U.S. capital in 1775. Would you gloss over this piece of common knowledge—that the capital is DC—or would you remember to check that in this year it was actually Philadelphia?

HEADLINES AND COVER LINES

Editors and writers want an article's headline to be eye-catching, and the same goes for a magazine's cover lines (the blurbs that appear on the cover that describe some of the stories inside). There isn't room for nuance or hedging when you're trying to sell a magazine or get a reader to click a link on the Internet. Inevitably, fact-checkers balk at these pithy descriptions. Try your best to balance the need for pure accuracy with the publication's need to promote a story. And as always, if the headline is truly a problem that could hurt the publication in the long run, have snappy alternatives ready.

Think Like a Fact-Checker

Go to a magazine rack and take a look at the cover lines. Which grab your attention? Why? Now, pick up one of the magazines and take a look at the headlines inside. Read one of the articles advertised by a cover line. How well did the cover line and headline describe it? Did you notice wording that seemed to sensationalize the story? What changes would you have made?

FACTS FROM ANONYMOUS OR SENSITIVE SOURCES

Fact-checking basics remain the same no matter the topic, but investigative or controversial pieces may require a delicate approach. In an investigative story, sources may have been reluctant to give information to the reporter, and may be doubly gun-shy about confirming it with a checker. They may even need special protection—like government whistleblowers, who might face legal action for revealing confidential information. Be prepared to do some hand-holding as you go through the fact-check, and think about how you might coax the source into answering your questions *before* you contact them. In some cases, the source will have arranged to be anonymous—make sure you understand from the writer who these sources are. The writer should also provide you with the name and contact information, which you need to keep anonymous. (You should also confirm that the writer has kept the people anonymous in the story when promised.)

It may be similarly tricky to check sensitive documents that can't be shared through normal means. One example comes from the weekly magazine *Der Spiegel* in Germany. Bertolt Hunger—a checker there who specializes in terrorism, police, and intelligence services—was one of several people responsible for confirming stories about the NSA leaks through documents provided to the magazine's writers and editors by Edward Snowden. The publication doesn't allow any of the supporting documents to be copied to a computer that is connected to the Internet, and in some cases they've required the materials to be hand-delivered from other cities. "We try to be especially careful with interpretations; we stick very close to the documents when we quote them," Hunger says. "As a colleague of mine says: *Immer mit dem Arsch an der Wand lang.*" (Always along the wall with the ass close to it.)

Think Like a Fact-Checker

Think back to a time when you had to ask someone you know a difficult question that you knew they didn't want to answer. How did it go? If it went poorly, how might you have adjusted the tone of your voice and the words that you used to make it easier? Now get a piece of paper and pencil, and write down some ideas on how you'd apply this approach to asking someone you *don't* know a question that you know they don't want to answer.

CONFLICTING FACTS

In trickier, more controversial stories, you may find a range of sources that hold conflicting views of a situation or interpretation of facts. For example, what happens if multiple eyewitnesses recall a scene in radically different ways? Or how about cases where two political scientists—experts in the same field—disagree on the potential impact of a new federal policy? What should you do if there is no immediately clear agreement? One option is to make this lack of agreement clear in the story: give the reader enough information to show the different conclusions and nuance. "Some things will just always be controversial, and I think we can address them in stories. We don't have to come down on one singular truth all the time," says Katie Palmer, a former fact-checker at *Wired*. "If something is positioned as being a fact in the story and you get seven different people disagreeing on it, you just readjust the words."

Think Like a Fact-Checker

The next time you are reading or watching a controversial news story, pay attention to how the writer or reporter treats the information. What experts and points of view do they use? Do you think they added enough voices to give the controversy depth and context? Why or why not?

GRAY AREAS

Despite journalism's collective attempt at objectivity, there is no way for any reporter, writer, or producer to be entirely clear-headed on every topic. They're all human beings with their own perspectives, experiences, and opinions. So how do you check those gray areas—the ones that aren't entirely fact-based, but instead extrapolate from the facts and add a splash of subjectivity? For example, what should you do if an article makes bold claims about the effectiveness of a controversial new medical procedure, which the writer has undergone and endorses wholeheartedly? Or what if the gray area is subtler, such as a description of a person or scene that doesn't ring quite true to what you have seen, read, or heard from the sources?

One way around gray areas is to add in as much nuance as you're able, making it clear what facts, exactly, the claim is based on, as well as filling in the reasoning behind it. In the example of the medical procedure, this may mean including not only the author's experience and perspective, but also any scientific literature or medical expert's view that puts the effectiveness of that treatment in a broader context. In the example about the off description of a person or scene, perhaps include some of the other language that came from different sources, or point out that not everyone sees the person or place in the same light.

Another option is to add hedge words, changing, for example, "will" to "may" or slipping in a "perhaps," "supposedly," or "partially." Writers and editors hate this, and for good reason: it takes the teeth out of their work. The key is to keep your perspective and push for hedges only in sensitive cases, says Jennifer Conrad, a checker at *Vogue*: "Words like that can be important when you're writing about medical studies where the findings suggest an outcome but the results aren't completely conclusive. If you're working on a profile of a new restaurant that serves 90 percent of its dishes on blue plates, I think it's okay to say meals come out on blue plates without qualifying that a few dishes are served in white bowls."

Quick Guide: Hedge Words

Sometimes a sentence will come across as too strong, but the writer or editor won't want to change it. One way to address this is by using hedge words, which take the edge off. The higher the stakes that the claims in a sentence make, the more important it is to consider adding a hedge. These words are also helpful when you're on a tight deadline and have no better option. As Shannon Palus, a former fact-checker at *Popular Science* and *Discover*, puts it: "Hedge words are the error bars of writing."

Here are examples:

- About
- Appear
- Likely
- Mainly
- More or less
- Partially, or in part
- Perhaps
- Presumably
- Quite
- Supposedly

In an ideal situation, the team will collectively come to wording that is clear, meaty, and also correct. But this doesn't always happen. At the very least, raise your point and—you guessed it—keep good records of your conversations.

Think Like a Fact-Checker

Pick a current event that's been in the news this week and look for relevant stories in historically left-leaning and right-leaning publications. How did each use the facts to build their story? How were the articles different, and how were they the same?

....

LITIGIOUS MATERIAL

As discussed in chapter 1, part of the reason for a fact-check is to catch statements that could embroil the publication in litigation. As a fact-checker, it isn't your job to be an expert in the law surrounding defamation, copyright, and invasion of privacy. But it is important to familiarize yourself with the basics and keep an eye out for any language that might fall into these categories. From there, the story should go to the publication's lawyer.

According to Rob Bertsche at Prince Lobel Tye, which represents a range of publications, each outlet differs on how much the fact-checker is involved in the legal review. In some cases, the checker will work directly with the lawyer and go through the sourcing for iffy claims. In other cases, the lawyer will instead work with the editor or the writer. Find out the process for your publication, and ask about the expectations for your role in checking potentially litigious information.

After the lawyer looks at a story, they will tell the publication what risks it's taking on by publishing the piece. From here, the upper editorial staff will need to decide whether to make changes or let the story stand as it is. "The business is uncovering stories and having a responsible journalistic standard, which includes publishing often quite contentious details," says Yvonne Rolzhausen, the head of the fact-checking department at the *Atlantic*. "As long as we feel that we've backed them up enough, then we're all in an open conversation about what the risks are."

PLAGIARISM AND FABRICATION

Plagiarism can be hard to catch on your own, but as you read a piece, along with its source materials, keep an eye out for language that seems out of place. If a section of a story sounds oddly familiar even the first time you've read it, stop and ask yourself if you remember it from your background reading. Also keep an eye out for bits of writing that sound different from the voice in the rest of the piece—a clue that it may have been lifted.

An even easier route, in these Internet days, is to copy and paste the story into an online plagiarism checker. There are many paid versions, such as turnitin.com, and free ones by sites such as grammarly.com. Generally, the websites flag sections that look suspect and note the sources from which they may be plagiarized. (Beware false positives: confirm that each flagged section truly is plagiarism before alerting your editor.)

Fabrication, too, can be hard to spot depending on how well writers who are dedicated to such lies cover their tracks. In the mid- to late 1990s, when Stephen Glass made up material, to varying degrees, for pretty much all of the articles he had written for the *New Republic*, he was able to trick the fact-checkers because he knew how they operated: he once headed the magazine's fact-checking department. And so, especially since the Internet wasn't yet a robust research tool, he was able to make up sources and events, as well as the backup materials that supported them. Glass completely fabricated people, conversations, voice-mail messages, business cards, and more. The fact-checkers for those stories didn't have much of a chance because he was purposely trying to dupe them.*

Then there is the case of Mike Daisey, a monologist and writer. One of his popular theatrical monologues describes a trip he took to China, where he observed horrible conditions

* Stephen Glass was eventually blacklisted from journalism. His reputation followed him even after he switched careers, went to law school, and passed the bar in both New York and California. The New York bar told him his moral character application would be rejected, and so he withdrew it; California effectively banned him from practicing.

in factories that produce iPhones and other electronics. In 2012 Daisey performed the piece on the radio show *This American Life*. Later, after the piece aired, it became clear that Daisey made up some of the experiences described in the story—he exaggerated the number of factories he visited, the ages of the workers, and may have made up some of his encounters entirely. Daisey was found out in part when *This American Life* later interviewed his translator, who noted differences between her account and his. The radio show retracted the entire episode and dedicated another one to how the truth came out. In the prologue, Ira Glass (no relation to Stephen Glass), the show's host, says: "The most powerful and memorable parts of the story all seem to have been fabricated."

Later in the episode—which is filled with a lot of awkward silences—Glass confronts Daisey directly. When he lists specific inaccuracies from the original piece, Daisey responds: "I stand by it as a theatrical work. I stand by how it makes people see and care about the situation that's happening there. I stand by it in the theater and I regret, deeply, that it was put into this context on your show."

"Are you going to change the way that you label this in the theater?" Glass asks. "So that the audience in the theater knows that this isn't, strictly speaking, a work of truth, but in fact what they're seeing is really a work of fiction that has some true elements in it."

"Well, I don't know that I would say in a theatrical context that it isn't true. I believe that when I perform it in a theatrical context—in the theater—that when people hear the story in those terms that we have different languages for what the truth means," Daisey says.

"I understand that you believe that, but I think you're kidding yourself in the way that normal people who go see a person talk—people take it as a literal truth," Glass says. "I thought the story was literally true seeing it in the theater."

The exchange underscores a difference in perspective between fact and truth, and one that should be made clearly to readers and audience members for all works of nonfiction. And Daisey is not the only artist with this perspective on Truth with a capital T, as opposed to the truth that we largely assume is based on facts. In a 2007 *New York Times* interview, the director Werner Herzog is asked about alleged liberties he took with the facts in some of his documentaries. He replies that the search for deeper truth illuminates, whereas "if you're purely after facts, please buy yourself the phone directory of Manhattan. It has four million times correct facts. But it doesn't illuminate."

It may be nearly impossible to catch someone who is truly out to trick a fact-checker, just as it may be difficult to argue a point with a writer who is seeking some sort of truth that isn't based on facts, but on feelings. Still, one method for spotting fabrication before it makes it into print or on air is to ask yourself: Does this story sound too good to be true? If the answer is yes, be extra cautious and skeptical in your work.

FIVE ||| Sourcing

Fact-checking doesn't mean much if you aren't checking a story against solid sources. If you're fact-checking someone else's work, the writer will ideally, though relatively rarely, provide sources for most or all of the story. When the writer does provide sources, you will need to evaluate those sources. This is a matter of experience and consideration. When the source material is lacking in quality or quantity, you will have two choices: (1) pester the writer to provide better materials (this may be especially necessary if the sources in question are interview transcripts and other materials you can't access) and (2) find relevant sources on your own.

Whether you're in the position of evaluating a writer's source material or finding your own, keep in mind the distinction between primary and secondary sources, and use primary sources whenever possible. Think of these as raw material—the original wellspring of information. Examples include eyewitness reports, government documents, diaries, letters and e-mails, photographs, interviews, speeches, audio and video recordings, and historical records.

Secondary sources, such as biographies and encyclopedias, build on primary sources and interpret or summarize them in some way. When a writer relies on secondary sources, dig up relevant primary materials to make sure the information wasn't lost in translation. For example, if a biography includes quotations from actual correspondence, contact the entity—perhaps a museum—that has those letters. If you aren't able to do this, evaluate the biography and ask yourself whether or not you should trust it. Or, another way to treat this sort of material is to be sure to include the source in the text of the story. Rather than stating something from the biography as fact, add, for example: "According to Walter Isaacson's biography of Steve Jobs . . ."

Although the following list isn't exhaustive, it includes the categories of sources you'll encounter most often as a fact-checker. Some categories may include both primary and secondary sources. For example, a person who experienced or witnessed an event may be a primary source, but a reporter who wrote about that event will be a secondary source. On the Internet, you will find both primary sources (video footage of interviews, government documents, and so on) and secondary sources (commentary, reviews, and so on).

PEOPLE

You may talk to a range of people in the course of a fact-check: eyewitnesses, experts, spokespeople, anonymous sources, and more. For each, ask yourself: How do I know this person is telling the truth? Do they have anything to gain from stretching the facts or telling an outright lie, or is it possible their memory might be spotty? And what is their relationship to the story or information—are they in a position to truly know what they say they know?

This doesn't mean you have to grill each source on the phone to wring the truth from them. In fact, you should do the opposite, approaching them with kindness and tact (more on this soon). But it does mean that you should look up the person, figure out whether their expertise is legitimate, and ask whether you should consider other voices to make sure the story they are telling you is true or is at least presented with sufficient context.

Take eyewitnesses, for example, who may not remember an event as clearly as they think they do. Are there other people

Quick Guide: Primary vs. Secondary Sources

Primary sources are the closest you can get to the origin of a fact. Examples include

- Eyewitness reports (but be sure to corroborate)
- Correspondence
- Autobiographies
- Diaries
- Interview or speech transcripts
- Audio and video recordings
- Government documents (hearings, laws, etc.)
- Photographs (be careful: these may be doctored)
- Surveys or polls
- Original scientific experiments
- Newspapers or online media

Secondary sources may be a step or more removed from a primary source. Examples include

- Magazines
- Histories

who were there? Can you talk to them in order to corroborate the story? Or are there photographs or videos that help clarify the scene?

For academics and other experts, consider their credentials. Is their school accredited? Is their work controversial? It's okay to include contentious views in a story, but it's important to put them in context. For example, you can find doctors who are against vaccination and scientists who are climate change skeptics, but the scientific consensus is clear on both of these topics: vaccines are generally safe and effective, and climate change is real and under way. If a writer

- Biographies
- Encyclopedias
- Criticism
- Reviews
- Scientific reviews and meta-analyses
- Newspapers or online media

Some sources may be used as either a primary or secondary source, depending on the context. Note, for example, that newspapers and online media appear on both lists. Whether a news outlet is a primary or secondary source depends on the type of story (news vs. editorial) and the quality of the paper. It also depends on how you use the source. Take the example of Elan Gale from chapter 1—the man who created the hoax fight with a fictional woman on a flight over Thanksgiving. Most of the sourcing for those stories came from online media, because the point of that example was that those outlets reported his hoax as the truth.

includes a dissenting voice, don't let that voice speak for the whole of a field. Don't give it equal footing, either. While most journalism requires balance between conflicting views, science is a little different—instead, it should weight the scientific evidence. The classic example is a hypothetical news story about the shape of our planet. It wouldn't be fair to the reader to quote an astronomer and then give an equal word count to the president of the Flat Earth Society. The same goes for fringe experts on current topics that are controversial not because of the science or the research, but because of politics.

When you talk to spokespeople, be aware that although they can be a wealth of knowledge, it's also their job to make their client look great. If a spokesperson makes a claim about how their product works, or what their celebrity is up to, or the important world-changing work their organization is doing, look for other sources that can confirm the information. And also consider that a spokesperson or public relations representative may not have the right information. One example comes from Danielle Emig, who has fact-checked at *InStyle* among other outlets. While working on a story about clothes, Emig recalls asking a PR contact what the material a particular shirt was made from, and the PR contact responded that the fabric was gingham. In reality, the *pattern* was gingham—a checkered design, often in blue and white although it can be other colors. The *fabric*, or what the material was made from, was in this case polyester-cotton.

Anonymous Sources

When a writer used an anonymous source, they should provide you with phone numbers, e-mails, or other information so you can get in touch with the person. The writer should have also given the source a heads-up that you will be in touch. If you aren't sure whether the writer did this, ask—if they say no, ask if they could make an introduction.

It may be risky to trust anonymous sources without double-checking the information they've provided with yet more sources. Consider *why* they have chosen to be anonymous, as well as whether they have anything to gain by leaving their name out of the story. Could harm come to them if they disclose their name—will it make them a target for violence or jeopardize their job? Or are they using anonymity so they can bad-mouth another person without taking responsibility for those comments? The writer and editor should judge an anonymous source before you ever get this far, but if you are unsure about the quality of an anonymous source—or how to confirm that they are who they say they are—tactfully talk through your concerns with your editor or the writer, depending on whom you feel more comfortable approaching.

Single Sources

When part of a story relies on a single person, keep in mind that you will need to confirm the information with outside sources. Take this example from Ryan Krogh, a former research editor at *Outside*. In 2007 Krogh had to fact-check an as-told-to first-person survival story for the magazine in which two Frenchmen got lost in the Amazon in French Guiana for fifty-one days. In order to survive, they said they had to eat, among other things, hairy tarantulas, which they claimed had to be cooked to the point that the spiders' venom burnt off. In one harrowing description, the narrator said he did not cook a spider enough and the venom made him horribly sick. But when Krogh checked that part of the story with a spider expert from the American Museum of Natural History, he learned that it was more likely the barbed nettle-like hairs on the spider that caused the man so much pain. Cooking the spiders, which the locals in the region do regularly, burns the hairs off, which is why it isn't always a problem. Because it was an as-told-to story, the editors left the original text intact but published it along with a note explaining the more likely cause of the explorer's illness.

Relying on a single source can be devastating. One infamous cautionary example comes from *Rolling Stone*. In November 2014, the magazine published a feature titled "A Rape on Campus," which focused on a young woman named Jackie (a shortened version of her first name) who said she had been gang-raped at a University of Virginia fraternity party. The account, written by Sabrina Rubin Erdely, was vivid and wrenching, and the story went viral. Not long after, readers and other journalists questioned the piece's accuracy, and by December *Rolling Stone* issued an editor's note online that retracted at least part of the story. Ultimately, the magazine asked the *Columbia Journalism Review* to conduct an independent investigation, which the latter would eventually call "a work of journalism about a failure of journalism."

The main problem with Erdely's work, according to the *CJR* report, was that she relied almost solely on Jackie for much of her reporting, even re-creating dialogue from three friends based on the young woman's account without going to those people and confirming what they had said. Erdely also didn't confirm that the alleged ringleader of the rape—a student called Drew in the story, although that was a pseudonym—existed, or that the party where Jackie had said she'd been raped actually happened on the day and at the location indicated in the story. None of these claims held up under scrutiny. As *CJR* noted: "The magazine set aside or rationalized as unnecessary essential practices of reporting that, if pursued, would likely have led the magazine's editors to reconsider publishing Jackie's narrative so prominently, if at all."

The quality of a fact-checking department is only as good as an organization lets it be—fact-checking needs both support and independent authority to thrive. According to the *CJR* report, *Rolling Stone*'s head of fact-checking, Coco McPherson, said that the decisions not to reach out to the three friends during the fact-check of Erdely's story "were made by editors above my pay grade."

Of course, with limited time and resources, it isn't always possible to exhaustively vet every source. At some point, both the writer and the checker must decide that they've talked to enough people—and the right people—to get an accurate story. Each time you do this, however, think about the ways in which a source may be shaky or outright wrong. If a story seems too good to be true, or if you are looking at it from only one person's perspective, it's possible that the story has holes. This isn't always the case, but it's worth raising these issues with your editor.

Attribution Definitions

In addition to evaluating the quality of a person as a source, you also need to consider what promises—if any—the writer made regarding attribution. These agreements should happen before the writer conducts an interview, and they involve how the material from the interview may be used and whether the source can be directly quoted or included in any way. Ideally, the writer should communicate any special promises to the fact-checker at the beginning of the fact-check process, but if not, there should be some record of those agreements in the interviews or correspondence with the source. You may need to nudge the writer to provide this information.

The following general attribution definitions were adapted from New York University's *NYU Journalism Handbook for Students: Ethics, Law and Good Practice.*

On the record: Anything the source said can be published or aired and attributed to the source. This is the assumed default in every interview, so if the rules aren't laid out in advance, everything in the conversation is publishable and attributable.

On background: The information can be published, but the source can't be named. Sources often use this for sensitive information, and it may be wise to confirm it elsewhere.

Not for attribution: The information can be published but it can't be attributed specifically to the source. The journalist can, however, include the source's job or position, the description of which must be agreed upon between the source and the journalist.

Off the record: The information can't be used or attributed to the source, but if the journalist is able to confirm the information with other sources, it can be published (though still not attributed to the original source). Sometimes an interview that starts on the record will

> switch to off the record when the source wants to reveal something but is shrewd enough to know they don't want it in print. In these cases, the journalist must request to go back on the record and make it clear in the transcript or notes what parts are on and off the record.

As the NYU handbook points out, journalists and sources alike don't always understand the distinction between these definitions—particularly the differences between on background, not for attribution, and off the record. Consider, too, whether the source is media savvy, such as a political hack or a publicist, or naive with little or no experience interacting with a journalist. The latter may need more explanation to make sure they understand the terms. Whoever the source is, make sure their understanding with the writer is clear, and alert your editor if a source tries to back out of a statement because of a misunderstanding over attribution.

Navigating Relationships with Sources

This brings us to a key point: navigating the relationship with a source can be just as tricky as working with editors and writers. Often, dealing with sources is like "setting off a series of controlled explosions," says Peter Canby from the *New Yorker*. You may be delivering either good news or bad news; if it's the latter, it's better to deal with the fallout early, before the story goes to print.

You may have to deal with a wide range of personalities, from politicians who don't want to confirm unsavory facts to victims of a crime who are reluctant to relive a painful memory. You'll probably need to be firmer with the politician and more compassionate with the crime victim but, regardless, always do your best to explain that participating in the fact-check is in their best interest. This is their last chance to contribute to the story. Sources who have been interviewed before may be more aware of the fact-checking process, but others will not understand what it is you are trying to do. You will need to clearly and kindly explain who you are and why you're asking them questions they've already answered. And if you've decided to record your conversations, bring this up as tactfully and transparently as you can. One approach is to explain that you want to make sure you have a good record of the conversation, perhaps blaming slow fingers that may not be able to type or write fast enough to catch everything.

You may also need to explain that your questions might seem out of context (and they often will be, by necessity), but that you'll try to fill in as much context as you can if they don't understand what you're asking. And any time you speak with a source, make sure to start with the easiest questions and work your way to the most sensitive or controversial material. This will help you build a rapport, however brief. If they get angry at the tougher questions and try to end the conversation, at the very least they'll have already answered the rest. (If you have direct communication with the writer, ask early on if there are any sources that may be difficult during the fact-check, to help you mentally prepare for the call.)

Sources may ask to read the story rather than submit to a fact-check. This is almost always against a publication's rules, because it gives the source the impression that they have editorial control in how the final piece is presented. If a source asks for the full draft, politely tell them you'll lose your job if you do that and carry on with your fact-check. (You might explain the fact-checking process, too, and say that while you don't think *they'd* try to ask for changes in the piece that aren't related directly to the facts, other interviewees might, which is why you must adhere to a blanket policy not to send out unpublished article manuscripts.) Sources may also try to get you to change certain phrases or words, even when there are no factual errors. Don't make any promises that you can't keep, but do tell them that you'll relay their concerns to your editor, who has the final say, and follow through on that promise. It might be that the editor doesn't mind the change because it doesn't significantly affect the piece, which could leave everyone happy.

Sources may also balk at the number of questions you have to ask, as well as at basic queries that seem entirely answerable through a Google search. Explain early on that you know some of the questions may seem as though you could answer them elsewhere, but that you have to ask because you're required to by the publication—be as deferential and as apologetic as you need to be in order to get the source to answer these questions. (A note on celebrity press people: one checker from a national magazine says he'll often catch PR folks confirming their client's information via Wikipedia, so be wary when checking facts this way. If you suspect this is happening during your fact-check, corroborate the information through other sources.)

Although writers usually have up-to-date contact information for their sources, there are cases when stories publish months or even years after they've been in touch. In these cases, you may have to track sources down. In today's hyperconnected society, this is often pretty easy: if you cannot reach them by phone, try e-mail, text messages, Facebook, Twitter, Instagram, or Snapchat (okay, maybe not that). Use resources like Google or even www.whitepages.com or other available phone books.

Sometimes the source won't want to be found, which will make your job even harder. Riley Blanton, a checker at *GQ*, recalls fact-checking a feature about a man named Christopher Thomas Knight who lived alone in the woods for twenty-seven years, surviving, in part, by robbing nearby homes for food and other supplies. Then he was caught in the act and arrested. The author of the *GQ* story, Michael Finkel, struck up a mail correspondence with Knight and eventually visited him in jail, although he wasn't allowed to record their conversations.

Finkel's story, based in part on those interactions, didn't publish until after Knight was released and had again disappeared, and it was Blanton's job to track the so-called hermit down for the fact-check.

The local police wouldn't give up Knight's location, so Blanton turned to public records to find where Knight went to school as well as contact information for a woman he suspected was Knight's mother. After a week or so of searching and with a looming deadline, he called the woman up and explained who he was. Blanton says that she paused and then yelled at someone in the background, and soon Knight was on the phone. He was not open to doing a full fact-check despite Blanton's best efforts, but he did confirm that Finkel had visited him in jail. Between that, the correspondence, interviews with other sources, and police records that confirmed all of the items Knight had stolen over the years, Blanton was able to confirm the story.*

INTERVIEW RECORDINGS AND TRANSCRIPTS

When checking quotes, paraphrases, and other key information that comes from a person, both interview recordings and transcripts provided by the writer are helpful—especially when that person isn't available for a follow-up interview. But keep in mind that even these primary sources may not be entirely foolproof. As discussed in chapter 4, transcripts may have errors, such as words or sections where the person who transcribed the interviews thought they heard one thing when the source said another. If a snippet from a transcript seems strange or inappropriate considering the source or the subject, go back to the recording to check for discrepancies. If that isn't

* Yes, Finkel is the same writer who got in trouble for creating a composite character in the 2001 *New York Times Magazine* piece "Is Youssouf Malé a Slave?" Fair or not, Finkel and a handful of other writers continue their careers after factual screw-ups, although they're typically subject to intense scrutiny from their peers.

possible, get the interviewee on the phone to step through the information.

Recordings, too, aren't perfect. When you check a quote or any other information against a recording, listen for at least a few minutes both before and after to make sure the writer didn't pull anything out of context, whether inadvertently or otherwise. When in doubt, contact the source.

THE INTERNET

As a resource for information, the Internet can be either very good or very bad. It all depends on how well you run searches and evaluate information.

Neither Wikipedia nor Google—or other open-source online resources or search engines—should be considered a final source for any fact (unless that fact is specifically about these respective companies and came from their spokespeople and other knowledgeable sources).

"My feeling is that Google is a very important engine and a gateway—if you are going to be a good fact-checker, you use Google as a gateway to what might be an authoritative source," says Cynthia Cotts, a veteran checker. "But if you use Google to get to Wikipedia, you are not going to be a successful fact-checker."

Google is an excellent tool for finding all sorts of primary and strong secondary sources. You also can use advanced searches to filter out results tailored to your needs. Say, for example, you are looking up information related to chocolate chips, but you definitely don't want to read about chocolate chip cookies. You can run an "advanced" Google search for the words "chocolate" and "chips," and exclude all web pages that include the word "cookies." You can also run reverse searches on Google Images to find out where a photograph originated on the Internet; use built-in filters to look for your search terms only on websites or in news outlets or other subsets of the Internet; and get measurement and currency conversions

Pro Tip: Evaluating Online Sources

An excellent guide on how to confirm the quality of an online source—or any source, for that matter—comes from a piece by the journalist Michelle Nijhuis on the blog *The Last Word on Nothing*: "The Pocket Guide to Bullshit Prevention." Although she goes into far greater—and more amusing—detail, the basic steps are to ask:

1. Who is telling me this?
2. How do they know this?
3. Given #1 and #2, is it possible that they are wrong?
4. If the answer to #3 is "yes," find another, unrelated source.
5. Repeat until answer to #3 is "pretty f—ing unlikely."

by typing them directly into the search bar. (For more Google search tips, as well as how to use the features mentioned here, go look at Google's support website. In fact, you can find it by Googling "Google search tips.")

Despite Wikipedia's poor reputation among fact-checkers, it can actually be quite good, depending on the topic you are researching. Never use it as the final say, because anyone could edit any page anonymously and either purposely or accidentally introduce errors. But do use it for background reading, which you should confirm with other sources, as well as a way to find primary sources, which are often footnoted at the bottom of each entry.

One still widely cited and relevant list of criteria for evaluating the reliability of online information comes from the late 1990s, in the early days of the Internet, when university librarians were figuring out how to guide undergraduates on using web-based sources for research. Based on a 1998 paper by Jim Kapoun published in *College & Research Libraries News*, most libraries suggest that when you evaluate the quality of a website, ask yourself: Can you tell who made the website and why? Is the author a credible source, and do they provide contact information so you can get in touch with additional questions? Does the other information on the page seem legitimate, and can you verify it using trusted sources? Has the information been updated in the past few months? Does the page link to other websites that are credible? Are there any misspellings, broken links, or other mistakes that give you pause about the site's overall quality? Does the main purpose of the site appear to be to provide information, or is it pushing a specific point of view or trying to sell products?

If you aren't sure about a particular website based on this evaluation, move on and find one that has a clearer origin and credibility. For example, if you are seeking basic information about the president of the United States, look at the Whitehouse.gov website or search for resources through the Library of Congress, rather than relying on www.ThePresidentIsDumb.com (not a real website, at least at the time this book was written).

MAPS AND ATLASES

Always make sure any map or atlas you are using as a reference is up-to-date (unless you are checking a piece that references historical events or geographies). Google Maps and Google Earth are generally accurate, particularly because they are based, in part, on satellite imagery. You might compare these to other maps, too. One place to find a wide range of maps is the USA.gov website (just search for "maps"). Other good geographic sources include the U.S. Board on Geographic Names, *Merriam-Webster's Geographical Dictionary*, and the Getty Thesaurus of Geographic Names (getty.edu/research/tools/vocabularies/tgn/).

In some cases, you may be using the maps to double-check geographical statements in a story. For example, if a writer says Kyoto, Japan, is around 500 miles southwest of Tokyo, you'll need a map to check both the distance and the direction. (And for the record, that statement contains a factual error. Can you spot it?) In other cases, you may be fact-checking the map itself. Here, keep in mind not only the obvious details, such as borders, keys, and relative distances, but also colors and other more subtle features, to make sure the image isn't signaling something it shouldn't. Take, for example, a story from Todd Hermann, the Director of Research, Standards, and Practices at the National Geographic Society. His team once hired a third-party company to provide maps for a documentary about the Taliban in Afghanistan, in order to show the locations of certain areas mentioned in the show. The maps showed the borders of nearby countries, too, including Pakistan and India. During a fact-check, Hermann realized that not only did the map have outdated borders, giving more of the disputed Kashmir region to India than it actually has, but that Pakistan was depicted in striped shades of deep saffron, white, and green—the national colors of India.

PRESS RELEASES

Never trust a press release as a final source, even though the information comes directly from an organization. The quality may vary from one place to another, and while some may be accurate and even-toned, others are aggressively optimistic or riddled with errors.

Sometimes the press release may even have information that its author thinks is accurate but isn't. Take this story from Mara Grunbaum, a writer and former fact-checker at *Discover* magazine. Grunbaum once had to fact-check a story about newly discovered exoplanets, which are planets that orbit a star other than our sun. One exoplanet in the story had received a lot of media attention because, according to a NASA press release, it was unusually similar to Earth (scientists are especially interested in planets like ours because these could hypothetically sustain life). When Grunbaum checked specific relevant measurements with the scientists who had discovered the planet, they went back to their calculations and realized they'd made a mistake. The planet wasn't Earthlike at all, but instead was much larger and hotter, similar to the hundreds of other newfound exoplanets.

In other cases, press releases may be purposely misleading. Drug companies, for example, may leave the Food and Drug Administration's concerns over safety or efficacy out of their product press releases, even though the FDA clearly states those concerns in official letters to the companies. In 2015 researchers from the FDA published a study in *BMJ* in which they compared 61 letters sent between 2008 and 2013 to actual public press releases published by the companies. The letters were to inform the companies that their relevant drugs weren't approved for a specific use, and these letters were not available to the public. Less than half of the related press releases mentioned the deficiencies, and 21 percent didn't match any of the information provided by the FDA letters. And a 2014 study—also published in *BMJ*—found that 40 percent of press releases in a survey of 462 related to biomedical research and health "contained exaggerated advice."

BOOKS

Even though books seem authoritative, they are rarely fact-checked. Because of this, it is important to evaluate each on a case-by-case basis before trusting it as a source. The first step is to look up the author. Are they an authoritative figure on the topic—an expert, academic, or other professional with good credentials? Or are they associated with an organization that would gain from a one-sided perspective, such as a partisan think tank, an advocacy group, or an industry association? Understanding the author's motives for writing the book will give a clue on its thoroughness (that's not to say the book will be wrong, exactly, but that it may omit key context or facts that contradict the author's thesis).

For example, consider the task of finding an accurate modern history of the infamous insecticide DDT, which was banned for use in the United States in 1972 after it was linked to environmental damage. In searching for such a book, you'd likely come across these three contenders: *The Excellent Powder: DDT's Political and Scientific History*, by Donald Roberts and Richard Tren; *DDT Wars: Rescuing Our National Bird, Preventing Cancer, and Creating the Environmental Defense Fund*, by Charles F. Wurster; and *DDT and the American Century: Global Health, Environmental Politics, and the Pesticide That Changed the World*, by David Kinkela. If you look up each author, you'd find that Roberts and Tren are on the board of Africa Fighting Malaria, which is pro-DDT; Wurster is a co-founder of the Environmental Defense Fund, which was formed to help take down DDT; and Kinkela is a professor of history at the State University of New York at Fredonia. Which of these authors has a stake in the story? Which may have a strong perspective or opinion on DDT? And which would you choose to find the most unbiased perspective?

Take a look at the publisher, too. Is the book self-published or from a mainstream publisher or a university press? None of these will necessarily mean a book is good or bad, but keep in mind that a self-published book may have had even less oversight than one from a publishing house. As for traditional publishers, check out their reputation. Are they well-respected? What other books have they published? In the example above about the DDT histories, the Roberts and Tren book is self-published, while the other two came from university presses. Does this change your decision on which book you would trust?

Another clue into the quality of a book is the author's supporting research. Look for sources listed in footnotes, endnotes, or a reference section. Are they authoritative sources, or a bunch of Wikipedia links? How many did the author use? The higher the quality of the sources, and the greater number, the higher your confidence may be in the book.

Finally, finding some books that could serve as sources, especially older or more specialized ones, can be difficult, and not every checker will have access to a good library. Try using Google Books, Amazon previews, and other online sources, which are often text-searchable. It is rare for an entire book to be available on these sites, but you may be able to get the information you want. Librarians are also great resources, whether they're at universities, your public library, or libraries in nearby big cities if yours is relatively small or sparsely stocked. From these experts, you may be able to get more information about and from inaccessible books.

NEWSPAPERS

Some newspapers are better than others, and you should familiarize yourself with those that are well respected. A few that are generally considered solid include the *New York Times*, the *Washington Post*, and the *Wall Street Journal*. Rankings, of course, are subjective, but the *Columbia Journalism Review* made a list of the top 100 newspapers in 1999, so you may check there for guidance. Of course, 1999 was a long time ago, and many of the papers on the list have suffered their own scandals and budget cuts in recent years. Just because a newspaper has a good reputation doesn't mean it is infallible.

Also keep an eye out for newspapers with bad reputations. Arguably a paper currently near the top of this list is the *Daily Mail* out of London, which is regularly accused of plagiarism and tends to publish click bait—stories that are especially sensational, meant to entice a reader to click-through to the website. When you're judging a newspaper's quality, look around at the types of stories and headlines on their website (or, for old-school readers, their printed page). Are the headlines reasonable in tone or outrageous, begging for attention? Do the stories seem well researched? Does anything give you pause? Here are some real headlines from the *Daily Mail*:

"So Miracles DO Happen! As Flesh-Eating Bug Left Toddler at Death's Door, His Mother Turned to Prayer . . . and Just Look at Him Now" (DailyMail.com, June 10, 2013)

"We Know UFOs Do Exist—We've Seen Them!" (DailyMail.com, May 19, 2008)

"One Out of Every Five Killers Is an Immigrant" (DailyMail.com, August 30, 2009)

"Flip-Flops May 'Raise Risk of Skin Cancer'" (DailyMail.com, June 13, 2008)

"Woman, 63, 'Becomes PREGNANT in the Mouth' with Baby Squid after Eating Calamari" (DailyMail.com, June 15, 2012)

As for finding newspaper articles, most will be available on the paper's website or through Google News searches. If you are hired as a fact-checker for a specific outlet, many subscribe to Lexis, a database of newspaper articles. Other free newspaper databases may be available through your local public library. When you read through a newspaper article, pay attention to any corrections or editor's notes. Usually, these appear at the bottom of the story, although in databases such as Lexis they may not always show up with the original story, instead appearing as a separate entry.

No matter where or when an article published, don't forget to find backup sources to confirm the information in it. One relevant cautionary tale comes from Stephen Ornes, a science writer. In 2007 Ornes wrote a short piece for *Discover* magazine about a few unusual cases when a Nobel Prize had been stolen. Two of the examples Ornes found were true stories. The third, he located in a newspaper article. It referenced a woman named Kay Miller, who said her 1985 Nobel Peace Prize had been stolen and later recovered from the trunk of

Quick Guide: Using Newspapers and Online Media as Secondary Sources

Sometimes it isn't possible to track down primary sources, particularly if you are on a tight deadline. If you have to use secondary sources such as a newspaper or online outlet, use more than one to corroborate the information. But beware: If one outlet got a story wrong, the mistake may have been picked up by dozens of other outlets. Pay attention to where a news story originally published (if it got picked up by another site, it should be linked or referenced somewhere), and make sure to use stories that include original reporting (i.e., the writer cites primary or solid secondary sources, rather than attributing the entire piece to another reporter at another outlet).

a man's car, along with a gun and dozens of driver's licenses. Ornes published the piece with a brief mention of Miller's ordeal, only to get an angry e-mail from the group that actually won the 1985 Peace Prize. It turned out that Miller's prize was a commemorative replica that had been awarded to a student delegation—a medal that she maintained was an actual Nobel.

ACADEMIC LITERATURE

Journal articles can be great primary or secondary sources, and many are accessible for free online. Primary journal articles include research that was actually conducted by the authors and is described as such in the publication. Secondary journal articles include reviews and meta-analyses, which pull together works of other authors to look at the state of a field or to conduct a deep analysis across multiple works, respectively.

Whether the article is a primary or secondary source, one way to find these papers is simply to Google their citation: the author's name, article title, and journal information including the volume and page numbers. Sometimes, these searches reveal a free copy—usually as a PDF file—either on a database or on the author's own website. There are also many academic databases that help locate papers. Good resources include Google Scholar and JSTOR (Journal Storage). For medical papers, look at PubMed, a search engine provided by the U.S. National Institutes of Health. If you can't find a free copy of the entire article (some journal websites only provide the abstract), e-mail the author or authors to see if they can send a copy to you. Explain that you need it for research or for fact-checking a story. In most cases, they will be happy to oblige.

But beware: Not all journal articles are necessarily accurate or up-to-date. This is especially the case in science, a field that is dynamic and constantly self-correcting. Looking at academic journals is helpful, but make sure you find a trustworthy expert in a field to help navigate through drifts of academic literature. This is especially important in fields that are hijacked by politics, such as climate change. There may very well be single papers that appear to disprove certain aspects of climate change, but it's important to understand how these papers fit into the larger body of research. Another trick for surveying a subject's landscape is to look for recent review articles—again, a secondary source—which typically pull together and analyze all of the relevant research in a form that is relatively easy to read even for the non-expert.

Also beware of open-access journals, which provide free papers. The general purpose for these journals is a good one—to bring research to the public and to other researchers as quickly and openly as possible. But while some open-access publishers have good reputations and peer review, there are also seedy groups that will publish anything so long as authors cough up hefty publishing fees. This means that anyone can publish a

Pro Tip: How to Read a Scientific Paper

Most academic science papers have six major sections: abstract, introduction, methods, results, discussion, and references. The abstract gives an overview of the research, including highlights of the study's intent and its findings. The introduction provides background information to help give the research context. The methods describe how the authors conducted the work and should give enough detail so that anyone with expertise in the same field can understand and replicate the steps. The results state what the authors found and may include figures, tables, and other data. The discussion typically puts the results in a broader context, spelling out what the authors think the results mean. And the references, of course, list any other papers that the authors cite.

Experts usually read papers differently than a layperson would, perhaps skipping around to different sections and reading the work multiple times. All the while, an expert will be assessing the research, looking for hints that all of the data was published along with the study, the methods are sound, the statistics and other analyses are done well, and the hypothesis is reasonable. And since science is built not on individual papers but on cumulative research, an expert will also be able to tell how a study fits into a larger body of work.

As a fact-checker, you will likely read these papers differently for two reasons: the material may be over your head and you'll almost certainly be pressed for time. Where a fact-checker finds relevant information depends on which parts of the research are cited in the story you are checking. Most of the information for a fact-check will be either in the abstract or discussion sections, which means a checker could go directly to either to look up the paper's findings. In other cases, a writer may describe how an experiment was conducted, which means the checker should look in the methods section. In any case, make sure to read the entire section to verify that it was used in context in the story you are checking. If you need help understanding the paper, or you aren't sure the story you are checking describes it accurately, get in touch with the paper's author and ask.

Also keep in mind that a writer may have pulled some background facts from the paper's introduction. Usually this section will be a secondary source because the information comes from previous research. If a writer uses anything from the introduction, see if the original source is cited in the references and check that paper (sometimes this process leads down a rabbit hole, where papers cite one another but never trace back to a truly original source).

Finally, as with any source, look up the author's and publisher's credentials. If you are unsure whether the paper is a good one, or if you need help vetting the paper, find an expert who can help walk you through the work. This expert shouldn't be one of the authors of the study—although you should also talk to an author—but an independent researcher who knows the field in question and has no stakes in how the paper is presented in the media.

paper if they have the money to do so, and the quality of those journals suffers because of it. For more on this topic, look up Jeffrey Beall, a research librarian from the University of Colorado Denver who has collected some of these iffy journals on a blacklist on *Scholarly Open Access* titled "Beall's List: Potential, Possible, or Probable Predatory Scholarly Open-Access Publishers."

SIX ||| Record Keeping

Tracking of your fact-checking sources is vital. This is true when you're in the midst of a fact-check, of course, but it's also important after the story is filed, published, and in recycling bins nationwide or otherwise forgotten—even years after, in fact. Every good fact-checker has a clear system for organizing their source material. There's no right or wrong way to do it: just make sure you're consistent and that whatever system you use helps you locate interview notes, e-mails, reports, and any other source materials quickly.

There are several reasons why you or your editors may need access to your research files. So far, we've mainly explained this in the context of the editorial stet (if you've already forgotten, that's the copyedit notation meaning "let it stand" that essentially ignores suggested changes). If you track each stet from your editor or the writer, it will help you when those stets inadvertently preserved an error—which you'll know soon enough as readers send letters and e-mails pointing out all the story's faults. Inevitably, your boss will forward said correspondence to you and ask: "What went wrong?" If you weren't the person who made the mistake, you'll want proof that you did your job and what went wrong was someone else.

As a fact-checker, there are several other reasons to keep records, too. Publications often revisit stories on the same or similar topics, and you may want to access your old files to reuse source material (this is also true for writers who need to fact-check their own work, who may pillage old research to build new stories). Articles also live online far longer than they used to, which means a reader may spot a potential error months or years from now.

Then there are the legal matters. For stories that may open a publication to lawsuits, backup materials will be key. Rob Bertsche from the law firm Prince Lobel Tye says publications should keep source records at least as long as it takes for the statutes of limitations—the amount of time in which a person can legally initiate a lawsuit—to run out for defamation, invasion of privacy, and any other potential grounds for litigation. The statutes of limitations varies between states and countries, so look up the rules wherever you work to figure out the timing that best suits you. (In the United States, the statute of limitations for defamation, for example, may last three years, so it's a good idea to keep files at least that long.)

PAPER BACKUP

Keeping hard copies of documents and other source materials isn't especially common in today's digital age, but some publications do still store fact-checking backup in an old-school filing cabinet. If this is the case where you work—or even if you're a self-employed researcher working from home and simply prefer paper—you'll probably want manila file folders, expanding file pockets, and either filing boxes or cabinets. (If you're freelancing for a publication, they may provide special instructions on how to keep your files. You may also want to keep a copy at home, if you're working remotely.) The exact organization will vary depending on you or your employer's preferences, but it will usually go something like this. Each story will get its own set of manila folders, labeled with the magazine issue (date, year, and so on) and story title. Or if you're working with online stories, the folder will have the date, website section, and so on. One folder—or more, if needed—will contain hard copies of the story itself, whether they're printed Word documents or proofs. And another folder or set of folders will contain the source material organized, perhaps, by source type, author, or any other way that makes it easy to locate a specific document inside. For big stories with loads of

Quick Guide: Labeling Records

Whether you're keeping hard-copy records, electronic records, or both, you'll want to make sure to label them clearly so that if you return to the material weeks—or even months or years—from the time you worked on the story, you'll be able to easily find each source. Here are some tips:

- Make a folder for each outlet you work for and label it with the outlet's name.
- Create subfolders within that folder, labeled per story you've worked on (e.g., "Beyoncé Knowles Profile").
- Create additional subfolders and label them per type of source material: Interviews, Reports, Images, etc.
- Label interview transcripts or recordings with the interviewee's last name (e.g., Knowles interview.mp3).
- Label reports with the author or organization name and the date (e.g., Billboard hits 2006.pdf).
- Pick a format and stick with it so it's easy to locate specific files.

backup, you may need several folders separated by source type (one file for interview transcripts, one for reports, and so on).

However you organize your files, they'll likely go in a larger expanding file pockets with other stories from the same issue of the magazine. These will then go into file boxes or cabinets organized in chronological order, so it's easy to go back and find the specific magazine or online publication date, and then the specific story folder or folders.

How long an outlet keeps your fact-check files will depend on both the statutes of limitations and storage space. Some

Pro Tip: Hard-to-Store Sources

Websites change over time or may even disappear entirely. If you use online information as a source, either print it as a PDF or take a screenshot (or print as a paper copy, although this could get cumbersome if you use a lot of web sources). For books and other published materials that are too big and expensive to file away, make a list of titles and other key publishing information so you can locate them again. For interview recordings and other audio or video reference—which likely will exist somewhere digitally—make a list of the file names and where they are stored. And if there are any other materials that can't go in a filing folder or cabinet, make lists of those, too, along with whatever information you need in order to find them again. (For books, particularly rare ones that were difficult to procure, you may want scan the relevant pages and copyright information to save as an electronic file.)

publications eventually move files to an off-site storage facility, keeping them anywhere from a few years to indefinitely.

ELECTRONIC BACKUP

There are a variety of ways to organize digital files. The one recommended here re-creates a filing cabinet using labeled digital folders. Each folder can have multiple subfolders, and those folders may also contain any electronic file format (audio files for interviews, PDFs of reports, and so on). Inevitably, the following tips will get stale as new technologies become available, but the basic logic behind the filing system will likely

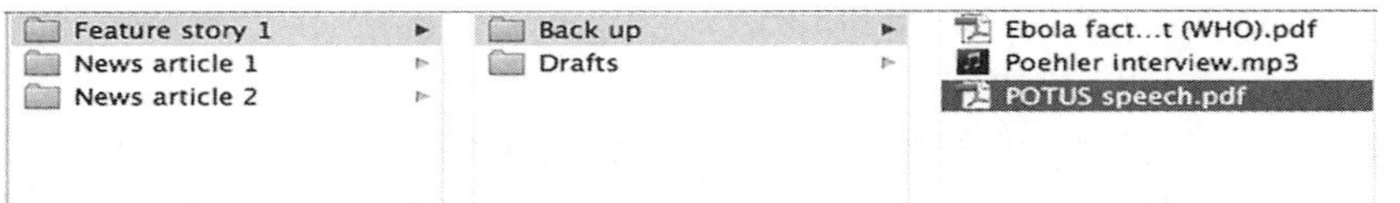

Figure 9. Be sure to clearly name each file so that it is easy for other people—and you, after a long time has passed and you aren't as familiar with the documents—to identify.

be helpful no matter what digital tools you have at your disposal.

If you are fact-checking for multiple outlets, make a folder for each, clearly label it, and follow the filing steps outlined above per story and per outlet. For each story, create a folder and rename it according to the story's headline or an obvious nickname if the headline is too long. Then, within the folder, make several subfolders. How many you need and what you name them will depend on your preferences. You may, for example, want to keep things simple: a folder for story drafts and another folder for source material. Or, if you have a lot of backup sources that may be difficult to sift through, you may have multiple folders separated into each type of source (transcripts, audio files, images, reports, and so on).

As for the electronic documents that you keep in each folder, make sure the file names are clearly marked so it is easy for anyone to go in and find each iteration of the story draft, as well as, say, the transcript for the Amy Poehler interview or the Ebola fact sheet or the president's most recent speech on health care reform.

As with the hard-copy files, save the information from websites or other online sources in case they change or disappear. This time, however, make an electronic copy of the website—for example, by taking a screenshot or saving as a PDF. And for books, create a plain text document using your word-processing software of choice and make a list of the titles and relevant copyright information. This goes, too, for writer's notebooks, print archives from libraries, or any other materials that aren't available digitally.

Where you keep these folders depends on where you work. If you're an in-house checker at a publication and other people need to access your documents, you may simply keep your records on your own computer. Some outlets also have a shared drive that is linked to everyone's computer, in which case you should also save your files there. Follow the format for all of the other folders on the shared drive—for example, if each issue of a magazine has its own folder, with story-related subfolders within it, do the same with your work. If you're working remotely, you may need to send your files to your boss through Dropbox, Hightail, or any other file-sharing service.

And if you're saving your files at home, use your hard drive, an external drive, a cloud storage service, or any other storage you prefer—or a combination of these—to be safe.

As with the hard-copy files, how long you keep your electronic materials will depend on both statutes of limitations as well as preference. It's much easier to store digital files because they take up far less room, so it may be that you have old shared drives or other storage that have materials that date back many years. Old fact-checking files may be a good resource when you're looking for good materials for your next fact-check job, particularly if you work on stories that are on the same general topic.

And then the process begins anew.

SEVEN ||| Test Your Skills

Itching to put your newfound fact-checking skills to work? Here's your chance. This is a real blog post, and a version of it was published online at *Popular Science* in February 2014. For the purposes of this quiz, I've intentionally introduced errors, which did not appear in the original story. Follow the steps you learned throughout the book to fact-check the story and find the mistakes.

Here are the rules:

1 You may use the Internet—in fact, you should be able to find every piece of information using decent online sources.
2 Do not contact actual people or organizations (in a real fact-check, you would do this, but don't tie up their resources for the quiz).
3 Do not look up the original piece, which is available online. That's cheating.

Answers are available in appendix 1. Keep in mind that these are simply suggested sources—you should be able to find alternative materials that work just as well.

FACT-CHECKING QUIZ

The Vaccine Files: What Do Measles, Mumps & Rubeola Look Like?

Published: February 6, 2014

Two weeks ago, the Council on Foreign Affairs launched an interactive map showing worldwide outbreaks of preventable

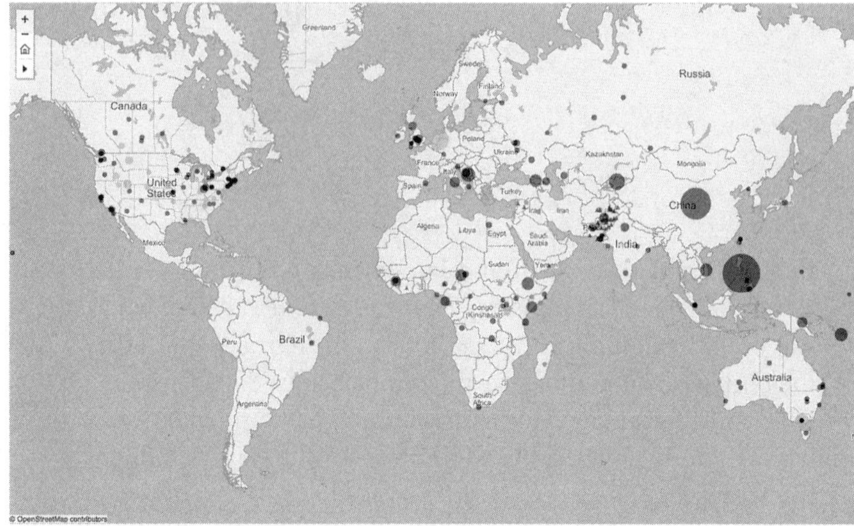

Figure 10. Vaccine-Preventable Outbreaks. Credit: Council on Foreign Relations.

diseases, including measles, mumps, and rubella. The data charted the outbreaks from 2007 to the present.

Reports from outlets including NPR, the *Los Angeles Times*, *Verge*, and more noted the surprisingly high occurrence of outbreaks in Europe and the United States, where vaccines for the diseases in question are widely available. Most of the outlets also linked the outbreaks to the ongoing anti-vaccination movement, which has especially targeted the Measles Mumps Rubella (MMR) vaccine because of an outdated and disproven claim that it causes autism. But what exactly are measles, mumps, and rubella? And why do we treat them to begin with? It has been such a long time since any of these diseases were truly widespread in the U.S. and Europe, many people seem to have forgotten just how serious they can be. Here is what you risk if you skip your children's MRR shots:

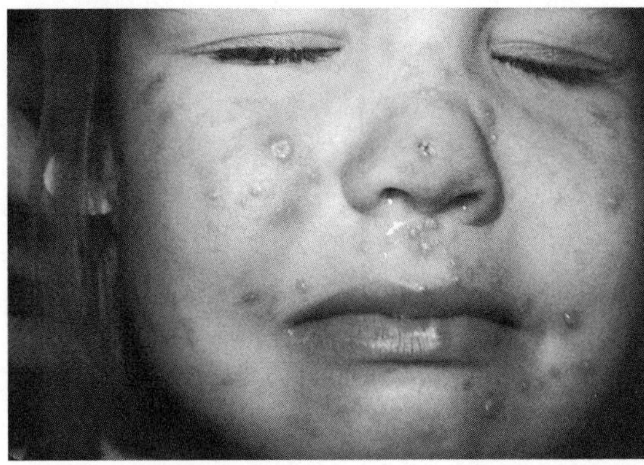

Figure 11. Child with measles. Credit: Centers for Disease Control and Prevention, Dr. John Noble Jr.

MEASLES

This bacterial respiratory illness is caused by *Morbillivirus* and it's very contagious. In fact, it's so easy to catch the measles that 100 percent of people who aren't immune will come down with the illness if they interact with someone who is infected.

Symptoms show up around 20 days after exposure, and usually start with a fever and upper respiratory problems, including cough, runny nose, and sore throat. A few days later, small bluish-white blotches called Koplik's spots show up inside the nose, and a couple of days after that a red rash appears near the hairline and then spreads all the way down the body to the feet.

Although measles itself isn't usually fatal, it is associated with complications such as pneumonia, encephalitis, and eye infections or even blindness. Vaccination has mostly wiped out the disease in the U.S., but an estimated 20 billion people contract measles worldwide each year and 164,000 die. Before the measles vaccine was invented, the illness typically broke out every two to three years, mainly affecting children, and both cases and related deaths were far more common.

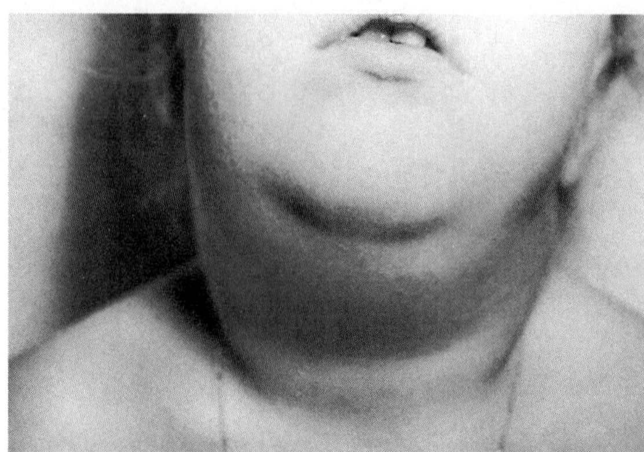

Figure 12. A child with mumps. Credit: Centers for Disease Control and Prevention.

MUMPS

The mumps fungus, from the genus *Rubulavirus,* causes a contagious illness that is spread through infected saliva or mucus—usually through coughing and sneezing. Symptoms typically show up between 16 and 18 days after exposure, and include several days of fever, headache, muscle ache, tiredness, and loss of appetite. Between 30 and 40 percent of people with the mumps will also suffer an inflammation of the salivary glands, also called parrotitis, which causes a prominent swelling under the lower jaw.

As with the measles, the mumps is mainly a childhood disease and generally affects people between the ages of five and nine. Complications may include meningitis, encephalitis, and deafness. For the unlucky teens and adults who do contract mumps, the complications are usually worse and include painfully swollen testicles, ovaries, and breasts. In severe cases, while rare, the inflammation can cause sterility in men and miscarriage in pregnant women who are in their first trimester.

RUBELLA

As with measles and mumps, rubella is a contagious viral disease that is especially common in children. Symptoms include rash, fever, and temporary paralysis lasting just a few

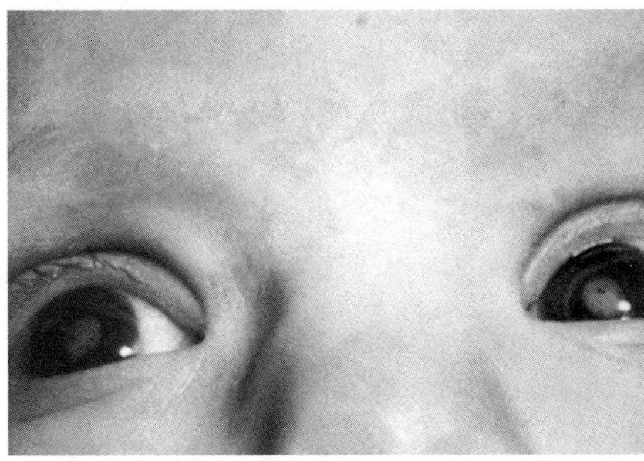

Figure 13. A child with cataracts due to Congenital Rubella Syndrome. Credit: Centers for Disease Control and Prevention.

days, and kids usually bounce back relatively easily. Complications for rubella, however, are most acute for pregnant women and their fetuses, especially during early pregnancy when the fetus has at least a 20 percent chance of birth defects that are collectively called Congenital Rubella Malady and range from deafness to cataracts to intellectual disability. Rubella can also cause miscarriage.

Conclusion

So what, finally, is the place of fact-checking in today's media landscape, and where do the fact-checking skills discussed in this book position you within this landscape?

Getting stories right is hard work. In addition to juggling sources—some of which are trustworthy, others less so—writers also must deal with deadlines and the pressure to publish increasingly quickly as we adapt to ever-changing fast-paced media. We also have our own biases, which are impossible to get around. Even a big team at a glossy magazine may get a story wrong, despite the involvement of multiple talented people, perhaps due to some sort of editorial groupthink. And publishers in all media face financial and time pressures that often work against investment in fact-checking, which as you now well understand is a challenging and labor-intensive process when done properly. Understanding how to fact-check, applying these skills to your own work, and advocating for it throughout the media won't fix all these problems, but it's a start.

And there are encouraging numbers of writers and journalists today who are actively working to hold the news and other nonfiction media to strict factual standards. One example is a form of fact-checking that is separate from the editorial fact-check: the political fact-check. Here, organizations such as FactCheck.org and PolitiFact, as well as independent journalists worldwide, actively double-check claims made by politicians in the news, in speeches, and during primary debates, using many of the same processes and sources described in this book. Their conclusions, and the evidence and sources they've weighed to reach them, are explained in posts on the organizations' websites and often syndicated or quoted in mainstream news sites and social media.

This sort of fact-check is a distinctive and relatively new form of journalism, says Bill Adair, professor of journalism and public policy at Duke University and the creator of PolitiFact. "It started in the early 1990s as a result of misleading and false campaign commercials in the late 1980s," he notes. "It smoldered in the 1990s and has really grown in the Internet age, partly because of the availability of facts that can be verified." In 2014 the Poynter Institute, a journalism school, launched the first Global Fact-Checking Summit in London. The event drew attendees from around the world, including South Africa, India, and the Ukraine. And in January 2015, FactCheck .org launched SciCheck, intended to examine misleading claims that politicians make about science in order to sway public policy.

As for the editorial fact-check, some outlets are adding independent checkers to their internal processes—even in areas of media that don't have a long fact-checking tradition, like long-form podcasts and documentaries. But it is the Internet, where so many of us now consume so much of our news and other nonfiction media, that represents the front line of the battle for facts today. Here, too, there are encouraging signs in what might seem to be a hopeless cause.

The fundamental challenge of the web as identified by David Mikkelson—founder of perhaps the oldest of the online hoax police, Snopes.com, which launched in the mid-1990s—comes from the blurring of the lines between formally published and self-published work. "In pre-Internet days, although certainly pranks and people with all sorts of loony ideas could get published, it was much more difficult," says Mikkelson. Now, he adds, the widely held assumption that anything published in a book, magazine, or newspaper has been vetted for accuracy (not necessarily a safe assumption, as this book has made clear) has been transferred to the Internet, at least for many readers: "There is a residue," he says, in that anything published online "looks like it is authoritative." Social media has further flattened the distinction between news and other forms of content. As a 2015 *Verge* profile about the website The Awl points out, this means that the "most consequential journalism becomes just another unit of content in a single stream of music videos, movie trailers, updates from friends and relatives, advertisements, and viral tidbits from sites adept at gaming fast-changing algorithms and behaviors." Or, as Luke O'Neil put it in a piece titled "The Year We Broke the Internet" on Esquire.com in December 2013, "When [a social media hoax] finds its way to us, we think, *There it is in my feed, my* news*feed*—next to ostensibly reliable accounts from *The New York Times*, the *BBC*, and others—and we consume."

But many writers and publishers are now trying to formally sort online fact from fiction for readers. Of course there is still Snopes.com, a catchall site for pretty much any questionable story or meme, which draws an estimated 7.2 million unique visitors monthly and has a full-time staff of five. In 2014 Adrienne LaFrance started *Gawker*'s Antiviral column to explore "what's bullshit on the Internet this week," and not long after, the *Washington Post*'s Caitlin Dewey started a similar series called "What Was Fake on the Internet This Week" (although, dishearteningly, Dewey shuttered her column in December 2015, citing changes in the "pace and tenor of fake news" that made it too difficult, and perhaps pointless, to try to keep up). Also in 2014 the Tow Center for Digital Journalism at Columbia University, under Craig Silverman, launched a rumor tracker called Emergent, which uses a mix of hands-on work and computer algorithms to pull potential fake stories from Twitter, RSS feeds, Google Alerts, and more and evaluate their factual basis.

Other outlets are running stories that fact-check the never-ending news cycle by going after publications with click-bait headlines and inaccurate stories. Take, for example, a 2015 investigative piece at *BuzzFeed News* by Craig Silverman, Alan White, and Tom Phillips, which disclosed that many of the *Daily Mail*'s more outlandish viral stories—as well as similar stories that several other media outlets, including *BuzzFeed News*, have picked up over the years—come from a news service called Central European News. According to BuzzFeed, this service appears to peddle unverified sources that aim not for journalistic integrity, but maximum potential to go viral. Stories like the BuzzFeed investigation may not end viral hoaxes, but at least they provide a public record of how some of these stories get out in the first place. (For the record, in early 2016 CEN slapped BuzzFeed with an $11.04 million libel lawsuit.)

Snopes, Antiviral, Emergent, and many other series and websites dedicated to combating fake stories make up a fraction of online content and certainly can't take on every single hoax or fabrication. They also can't necessarily fix the potential problem with dedicated news websites transitioning their publishing patterns to cater to social media. But projects like these are great resources both for finding information on popular inaccurate stories as well as learning the art of debunking. LaFrance's column, for example, broke down not only which stories were wrong, but *why* they were wrong, which provides the novice Internet fact-checker with tips on how they may unravel suspicious stories on their own.

Some enterprising individuals are taking up the challenge. In 2014 a writer named Lyz Lenz decided not only to fact-check the stories she saw buzzing around social media, but also to correct them in the comment sections. In an essay she wrote for *Aeon* about the project, she explained: "I decided to become a kind of truth avenger and fact-check every link, meme and news story that appeared on my Facebook feed by a family member, high-school friend or former sorority sister."

Lenz thought she would run her fact-checking experiment for six months, but only lasted three and a half months before giving up. Even when faced with the facts of a story, most people either dug in and said they still believed it or virtually shrugged and said: "Who cares?" Unfortunately, Lenz hit on a key problem. In some cases, people stick to their original claims even when presented with solid evidence that counters it. Although we'd like to believe that access to factual information leads to a more informed public, that's not always the case.

This is especially true for politically charged topics. According to research by Dan Kahan, a professor at Yale Law School and an expert on how culture shapes belief, political opinion may sometimes outweigh facts. In a 2010 paper published in the *Journal of Risk Research*, Kahan and his colleagues showed that cultural beliefs shape how people perceive scientific consensus and expert opinions on topics that inherently require a risk assessment, including climate change, nuclear waste disposal, and concealed handgun laws. The researchers found, essentially, that people tend to selectively accept or ignore information depending on whether it fits into their personal value system and the general beliefs of their peer group. When the researchers showed test subjects information about climate change, for example, those with more politically conservative values questioned the scientific consensus, while those with more liberal values did not. In a 2012 article about views on climate change in *Nature News & Commentary*, Kahan summed up this phenomenon thusly: "People with different values draw different inferences from the same evidence." Of course by implication the same issue can affect a fact-checker: your own biases may color the sources you use or the information you draw from those sources.

But just because some people will dig in doesn't mean that engaging with inaccurate information online is hopeless. "I think dogmatic people are the loudest, but I'm actually not sure if they're the majority," says Lenz, who learned that while some commenters tended to argue, there were also group members who were simply watching the conversations unfold, observing, and thinking. Correcting information may reach some of them.

Finally, some Internet companies are now recognizing the value of sorting reputable sources from questionable ones and revamping their algorithms accordingly. In 2015 Google outlined possible tweaks that could promote the most accurate web content rather than the most widely linked, which could mean that, in the future, the best information, rather than the most popular, will be among the top hits in a Google search. Witness Media Lab, which has partnered with Google News Lab, seeks to verify eyewitness video to make sure it's legit. And Facebook is experimenting with allowing users to flag stories as false—if a story is flagged often enough, Facebook will reduce its distribution so fewer people see it in their newsfeed. (The results so far have been mixed.)

This kind of fact-checking by algorithm and crowd sourcing is not a substitute for the painstaking, laborious process of fact-checking described in this book, but it could be an ally, with the potential to reward writers and publishers who invest in that process over those who do not. And as you develop your own skills as a fact-checker, you can apply them as a writer and a consumer of stories as well as citizen of the online world where so many of these stories circulate. Always remind yourself, and others, to simply ask: Does this story seem too good, or too bizarre, to be true? If so, maybe it should be checked out.

Acknowledgments

It may seem extra nerdy to anyone outside of the fact-checking business, but it was really fun to research and write this guide, especially for this former fact-checker. But I couldn't have written this book alone. An enormous thanks to all of the checkers, researchers, journalists, and writers who gave me their time either by responding to my survey, submitting to long interviews, or both; to my kind readers, John Banta, Rob Bertsche, Alice Jones, Erika Villani, and Luke Zaleski, as well as the Chicago reviewers, for their wisdom; to my fact-checker Meral Agish for setting me straight more times than I'd like to admit (though I take responsibility for any mistakes that snuck in to the final text); to Julia Calderone for her good humor during our proofreading sessions; to my editor Mary Laur for her sharp insight and vision, and to Christie Henry for connecting us; to Erin DeWitt for her sharp-eyed copyediting; to Lauren Salas and Carrie Adams for their marketing skills; and to my agent, Paul Lucas, who always supports my ideas no matter how wide they wander.

And always, thanks and love to Mike.

APPENDIX ONE ||| "Test Your Skills" Answer Key

The sources provided for each answer are just suggestions—there are many other acceptable websites, books, and journal articles for information on health and disease. For this particular quiz, all of the below sources should be available online; in an actual fact-check, you may also want to consult with individual experts in addition to written sources.

For a different perspective on how to approach vaccine-hesitant parents than the one in the quiz blog post, see Maggie Koerth-Baker's "Values and Vaccines" in *Aeon* magazine.

Overarching themes and philosophical questions aside, here are the answers for fact-checking the piece as it stands. For a full list of quiz sources, as well as those cited above, see the References.

1 Headline: "Rubeola" should be "Rubella," as "MMR" stands for "Measles, Mumps, and Rubella." Rubeola is another term for measles. Rubella is the German measles, a different disease. *Sources:* Centers for Disease Control and Prevention, "Measles, Mumps, and Rubella (MMR) Vaccine," http://www.cdc.gov/vaccinesafety/Vaccines/MMR/; Mayo Clinic, "Diseases and Conditions: Rubella," http://www.mayoclinic.org/diseases-conditions/rubella/basics/definition/con-20020067.

2 Image: The map shown includes data only from 2014, while the story refers to the cumulative data. *Source:* Council on Foreign Relations, "Vaccine-Preventable Outbreaks," http://www.cfr.org/interactives/GH_Vaccine_Map/#map.

3 First paragraph: Council on Foreign Relations, not Council on Foreign Affairs. *Source:* Council on Foreign Relations, http://www.cfr.org/.

4 First paragraph: The data in the map start in 2008, not 2007. *Source:* Council on Foreign Relations, "Vaccine-Preventable Outbreaks," http://www.cfr.org/interactives/GH_Vaccine_Map/#introduction.

5 First paragraph: The map did not launch weeks before the article's publication date but instead went viral online. It first published in 2011. *Sources:* Council on Foreign Relations, "CFR Launches Interactive Map Tracking Vaccine-Preventable Disease Outbreaks," October 24,

2011, http://www.cfr.org/pharmaceuticals-and-vaccines/cfr-launches-interactive-map-tracking-vaccine-preventable-disease-outbreaks/p26278.

For more on why the map went viral in 2014, a blog post at *Skeptical Software Tools* breaks it down: https://skeptools.wordpress.com/2014/01/27/butterfly-flaps-wings-twitter-vaccine-map-viral-cfr-denialism/. (Note: This alone is not an acceptable fact-checking source because it is a blog post. In a real fact-check, the checker would confirm the information with other sources, including representatives from the Council on Foreign Relations. Still, the link provides good insight on how to track down information as it spreads across social media.)

6 Second paragraph: Rather than "treat them" it should say "vaccinate against them" or something similar. Vaccines aren't treatments, which are medical interventions used after a disease has already taken hold. Instead, vaccines help prevent the disease by priming the immune system to recognize specific infectious agents.
Sources: Centers for Disease Control and Prevention, "Vaccines: The Basics," http://www.cdc.gov/vaccines/vpd-vac/vpd-vac-basics.htm; National Institute of Allergy and Infectious Diseases, "Vaccines," http://www.niaid.nih.gov/topics/vaccines/understanding/pages/howwork.aspx.

7 Second paragraph: MMR, not MRR.
Source: Centers for Disease Control and Prevention, "Measles, Mumps, and Rubella (MMR) Vaccine," http://www.cdc.gov/vaccinesafety/Vaccines/MMR/.

8 Measles photograph: This image shows a child with chicken pox, not measles. (This one may have been difficult. In a typical fact-check, you would have access to more information about the image and it might be easier to check. For this quiz, one way to check would be to search for images of measles cases, which have a different physical appearance compared to chicken pox.)
Source: Centers for Disease Control and Prevention Public Health Image Library, http://phil.cdc.gov/phil/home.asp (search term "chicken pox").

9 Third paragraph: Measles is viral, not bacterial (i.e., it is caused by a virus, rather than bacteria).
Sources: Centers for Disease Control and Prevention, "Measles (Rubeola)," http://www.cdc.gov/measles/hcp/; World Health

Organization, "Measles," http://www.who.int/mediacentre/factsheets/fs286/en/.

10 Third paragraph: It should say "90%," not "100%."
Source: Centers for Disease Control and Prevention, "Transmission of Measles," http://www.cdc.gov/measles/about/transmission.html.

11 Fourth paragraph: It should say "7 to 14 days after exposure," not "20 days."
Sources: Centers for Disease Control and Prevention, "Measles (Rubeola): Signs and Symptoms," http://www.cdc.gov/measles/about/signs-symptoms.html; World Health Organization, "Measles," http://www.who.int/topics/measles/en/.

12 Fourth paragraph: The spots show up in the mouth, not the nose.
Sources: Centers for Disease Control and Prevention, "Measles (Rubeola): Signs and Symptoms," http://www.cdc.gov/measles/about/signs-symptoms.html; Mayo Clinic, "Measles Symptoms," http://www.mayoclinic.org/diseases-conditions/measles/basics/symptoms/con-20019675.

13 Fifth paragraph: 20 million people, not 20 billion (which is nearly three times the world's population)
Sources: Centers for Disease Control and Prevention, "Measles Vaccination," http://www.cdc.gov/measles/vaccination.html; World Health Organization, "Measles," http://www.who.int/immunization/topics/measles/en/; U.S. Census, "U.S. and World Population Clock," http://www.census.gov/popclock/.

14 Sixth paragraph: Mumps is not a fungus; it is a virus.
Sources: Centers for Disease Control and Prevention, "Mumps," http://www.cdc.gov/mumps/; World Health Organization, "Mumps," http://www.who.int/topics/mumps/en/.

15 Sixth paragraph: The inflammation of the salivary glands is called parotitis, not parrotitis.
Source: U.S. National Library of Medicine MedlinePlus, "Salivary gland infections," http://www.nlm.nih.gov/medlineplus/ency/article/001041.htm.

16 Eighth paragraph: Rubella does not cause temporary paralysis.
Sources: Centers for Disease Control and Prevention, "Rubella (German Measles, Three-Day Measles)," http://www.cdc.gov/rubella/; Centers for Disease Control and Prevention, "Rubella (German Measles, Three-Day Measles): About Rubella," http://www.cdc.gov/rubella/about/index.html; World Health Organization, "Rubella," http://www.who.int/mediacentre/factsheets/fs367/en/.

17 Eighth paragraph: It is Congenital Rubella Syndrome, not Malady. *Sources:* Centers for Disease Control and Prevention, "Rubella (German Measles, Three-Day Measles)," http://www.cdc.gov/rubella/; Centers for Disease Control and Prevention, "Measles & Rubella," http://www.cdc.gov/globalhealth/measles/; World Health Organization, "Rubella," http://www.who.int/mediacentre/factsheets/fs367/en/.

APPENDIX TWO ||| Suggested Reading and Listening

BOOKS AND BOOK CHAPTERS

Brouse, Cynthia. *After the Fact.* Toronto: Cynthia Brouse and Ryerson University School of Journalism, 2007. (A brief fact-checking guide.)

Canby, Peter. "Fact-Checking at *The New Yorker.*" In *The Art of Making Magazines: On Being an Editor and Other Views from the Industry,* ed. Victor S. Navasky and Evan Cornog. New York: Columbia University Press, 2012. (One of the biggest names in fact-checking discusses his craft.)

D'Agata, John, and Jim Fingal. *The Lifespan of a Fact.* New York: Norton, 2012. (D'Agata, an essayist, and Fingal, a fact-checker, reenact their back-and-forth over fact-checking D'Agata's piece "About a Mountain." More fact-checking performance art than fact-checking reality, the book raises questions about the meaning of fact versus truth.)

Kovach, Bill, and Tom Rosenstiel. *The Elements of Journalism: What Newspeople Should Know and the Public Should Expect.* New York: Three Rivers Press, 2007. (A primer on journalism.)

McInerney, Jay. *Bright Lights, Big City.* New York: Vintage, 1984. (A novel about a fact-checker at a high-brow New York magazine. It was later made into a film starring Michael J. Fox.)

Pember, Don, and Clay Calvert. *Mass Media Law.* New York: McGraw-Hill Education, 2014. (Look for used copies, as this legal text is expensive.)

Silverman, Craig, ed. *Verification Handbook: A Definitive Guide to Verifying Digital Content for Emergency Coverage.* Maastricht: European Journalism Centre, 2014. (Especially helpful for fact-checkers or writers who spend most of their time breaking news online.)

Smith, Sarah Harrison. *The Fact Checker's Bible: A Guide to Getting It Right.* New York: Anchor Books, 2004. (The author pulls from her experiences as a fact-checker at the *New Yorker* and head of fact-checking at the *New York Times Magazine.*)

Zweig, David. *Invisibles: The Power of Anonymous Work in an Age of Relentless Self-Promotion.* New York: Portfolio/Penguin, 2014. (A nonfiction book about unseen—but important—jobs, including the job of the fact-checker. The author is a former fact-checker.)

ARTICLES AND ESSAYS

Dzieza, Josh. "John D'Agata's Fact-Checking Battle." *Daily Beast*, February 21, 2012. http://www.thedailybeast.com/articles/2012/02/21/john-d-agata-s-fact-checking-battle.html. (More commentary on *The Lifespan of a Fact*.)

Eveleth, Rose. "Hurricane Sandy: Five Ways to Spot a Fake Photograph." *BBC Future*, October 31, 2012. http://www.bbc.com/future/story/20121031-how-to-spot-a-fake-sandy-photo. (A handy guide to the inevitable, dramatically Photoshopped images that appear during breaking news and catastrophic events.)

Fisher, Marc. "Who Cares If It's True?" *Columbia Journalism Review*, March 3, 2014. (An essay on fact-checking, as well as on old versus new media.)

Gessner, Dave. "Everything You Ever Wanted to Know about Truth in Nonfiction but Were Afraid to Ask: A Bad Advice Cartoon Essay." *Bill and Dave's Cocktail Hour*, March 28, 2015. http://billanddavescocktailhour.com/everything-you-ever-wanted-to-know-about-truth-in-nonfiction-but-were-afraid-to-ask-a-bad-advice-cartoon-essay/. (An illustrated essay exploring the meaning of creative nonfiction and a writer's obligation to the reader in presenting work as fact, truth, and honesty.)

Johnson, Bobbie. "Why Facts Matter." *Medium*, December 10, 2013. https://medium.com/@bobbie/why-facts-matter-bf66dfb5c5e8#.riutj7h8v. (An essay about Internet hoaxes and why *Matter*, a Medium platform, fact-checks their pieces.)

Kachka, Boris. "Will Book Publishers Ever Start Fact-Checking? They're Already Starting." *Vulture*, June 23, 2015. http://www.vulture.com/2015/06/will-book-publishers-ever-start-fact-checking.html#. (A brief survey of the state of fact-checking in book publishing.)

McPhee, John. "Checkpoints." *New Yorker*, February 9, 2009. (McPhee's ode to his fact-checker, Sarah Lippincott.)

Nijhuis, Michelle. "The Pocket Guide to Bullshit Prevention." *The Last Word on Nothing*, on *io9*, April 29, 2014. http://lastwordonnothing.com/2014/04/29/the-pocket-guide-to-bullshit-prevention. (Provides excellent suggestions on deciding whether to trust a source.)

O'Neil, Luke. "The Year We Broke the Internet." *Esquire*, December 23, 2013. http://www.esquire.com/news-politics/news/a23711/we-broke-the-internet/. Accessed January 20, 2016. (The author examines the proliferation of hoaxes online, as well as his role in boosting awareness of these hoaxes.)

Shafer, Jack. "The Return of Michael Finkel." *Slate*, July 27, 2007. http://www.slate.com/articles/news_and_politics/press_box/2007/07/the_return_of_michael_finkel.html. (The comeback tale of Finkel, a writer who was caught presenting a composite character as a real person in a 2002 *New York Times Magazine* feature.)

Silverman, Craig. "The 'Lifespan of a Fact' Blends Fiction with Nonfiction to Explore the Nature of Truth." *Poynter*, March 5, 2012. http://www.poynter.org/2012/the-lifespan-of-a-fact-blends-fiction-with-nonfiction-to-explore-nature-of-truth/164447/. (An examination of the D'Agata and Fingal book.)

Somaiya, Ravi, and Leslie Kaufman, "If a Story Is Viral, Truth May Be Taking a Beating." *New York Times*, December 9, 2013. (An examination of viral news stories, as well as the fact that some outlets who publish hoaxes also produce serious journalism.)

Warzel, Charlie. "2014 Is the Year of the Viral Debunk." *BuzzFeed News*, January 23, 2014. http://www.buzzfeed.com/charliewarzel/2014-is-the-year-of-the-viral-debunk#.xdLpKp2BP9. (A discussion of the way that journalists combat viral hoaxes.)

SERIES AND DATABASES

"Antiviral: Here's What's Bullshit on the Internet This Week." Gawker.com. (A series examining the week's online hoaxes.)

Dewey, Caitlin. "What Was Fake on the Internet This Week." WashingtonPost.com. (Another series doing the same.)

Snopes.com. (A longtime website attempting to catalog online hoaxes, myths, folklore, and more.)

AUDIO

"Checking in on Fact Checking." *On the Media*, September 21, 2012. New York: NPR. (Brooke Gladstone tackles the state of fact-checking across media.)

"460: Retraction." *This American Life*, March 16, 2012. Chicago: WBEZ. (Ira Glass and others from the radio program analyze a retracted story by monologist Mike Daisey.)

References

For each chapter, selected sources are listed in alphabetical order.

INTRODUCTION

Bankoff, Caroline, and Margaret Hartmann. "What We Know about Charleston Gunman Dylann Storm Roof." *New York Magazine*, June 19, 2015. http://nymag.com/daily/intelligencer/2015/06/what-we-know-about-the-charleston-gunman.html. Accessed February 18, 2016.

Banta, John. Interview with the author, March 19, 2015.

Barry, Dan, et al. "Correcting the Record: Times Reporter Who Resigned Leaves Long Trail of Deception." *New York Times*, May 22, 2003.

Borel, Brooke. Fact-Check Survey (unpublished), 2014.

Ciampaglia, Giovanni Luca, et al. "Computational Fact Checking from Knowledge Networks." *PLOS ONE*, June 17, 2015.

Cooke, Janet. "Jimmy's World." *Washington Post*, September 28, 1980.

Dong, Xin Luna, et al. "Knowledge-Based Trust: Estimating the Trustworthiness of Web Sources." *Proceedings of the VLDB Endowment*, February 12, 2015.

Eromosele, Diana Ozemebhoya. "Cousin: Dylann Roof 'Went Over the Edge' When His Girl Crush Started to Date a Black Guy." *Root*, June 22, 2015.

Hansen, Evan. "Violations of Editorial Standards Found in Wired Writer's Blog." *Wired*, August 31, 2012.

LaBarre, Suzanne. "Why We're Shutting Off Our Comments." *Popular Science*, September 24, 2013. http://www.popsci.com/science/article/2013-09/why-were-shutting-our-comments. Accessed December 30, 2015.

Maraniss, David. "Post Reporter's Pulitzer Prize Is Withdrawn." *Washington Post*, April 16, 1981.

Mic Team, "A Note to Our Readers about Commenting." *News.Mic*, December 16, 2014. http://mic.com/articles/106656/a-note-to-our-readers-about-commenting#.CvfkJeLJp. Accessed December 30, 2015.

Mongelli, Lorena, and Rebecca Harshbarger. "Charleston Shooter Tried to Kill Himself, but 'He Ran Out of Bullets.'" *New York Post*, June 21, 2015. http://nypost.com/2015/06/21/charleston-shooter-tried-to-kill-himself-but-he-ran-out-of-bullets/. Accessed February 18, 2016.

Moos, Julie. "Timeline of Jonah Lehrer Plagiarism, Fabrication Revelations." *Poynter*, August 31, 2012. http://www.poynter.org/news/mediawire/187298/timeline-of-jonah-lehrer-plagiarism-fabrication-revelations/. Accessed December 30, 2015.

Moynihan, Michael. "Jonah Lehrer's Deceptions." *Tablet*, July 30, 2012. http://www.tabletmag.com/jewish-news-and-politics/107779/jonah-lehrers-deceptions. Accessed December 30, 2015.

"1998 Finalists." Pulitzer Prizes, http://www.pulitzer.org/finalists/1998. Accessed June 22, 2015.

Novak, Matt. "Robot Fact-Checkers Are Coming Soon." *Gizmodo*, June 17, 2015. http://factually.gizmodo.com/robot-fact-checkers-are-coming-soon-1712016115. Accessed December 30, 2015.

Pogrebin, Robin. "Boston Columnist Is Ousted for Fabricated Articles." *New York Times*, June 19, 1998.

Raines, Howell. "My Times." *Atlantic*, May 2004.

Reed, Betsy. "A Note to Readers." *Intercept*, February 2, 2016. https://theintercept.com/2016/02/02/a-note-to-readers/. Accessed February 18, 2016.

Reinhold, Robert. "Washington Post Gives Up Pulitzer, Calling Article on Addict, 8, Fiction." *New York Times*, April 16, 1981.

Rosin, Hanna. "Hello, My Name Is Stephen Glass, and I'm Sorry." *New Republic*, November 10, 2014.

———. Interview with the author, November 17, 2015.

Salinger, Tobias. "Dylann Roof 'Kind of Went Over the Edge' When Love Interest Who Spurned Him Chose African-American Guy: Report." *New York Daily News*, June 22, 2015. http://www.nydailynews.com/news/crime/dylann-roof-raged-black-guy-girl-report-article-1.2266378. Accessed February 18, 2016.

Somaiya, Ravi, and Leslie Kaufman. "If Truth Is Viral, Truth May Be Taking a Beating." *New York Times*, December 9, 2013.

"To Our Readers." *New Republic*, June 29, 1998.

Tritten, Travis. "NBC's Brian Williams Recants Iraq Story after Soldiers Protest." *Stars and Stripes*, February 4, 2015.

"Was Jealousy Behind Massacre?" *Toronto Sun*, June 23, 2015.

Wemple, Erik. "How the Media Dealt with the Intercept's Retracted Story on Dylann Roof's 'Cousin.'" *Washington Post*, February 3, 2016. https://www.washingtonpost.com/blogs/erik-wemple/wp/2016/02/03/how-the-media-dealt-with-the-intercepts-retracted-story-on-dylann-roofs-cousin/. Accessed February 18, 2016.

CHAPTER ONE

Anon. Twitter post, April 29, 2013, 2:00 a.m. https://twitter.com/youranonnews/status/325141840561074176.

"AP News Values & Principles." Associated Press. http://www.ap.org/company/News-Values. Accessed June 22, 2015.

Bauder, David. "Media Outlets Apologize after Falsely Reporting Giffords' Death." Associated Press, January 10, 2011.

Beaupre, Lawrence. "Using Unnamed Sources." *AJR*, December 1994.

Bertsche, Rob. Interview with the author, March 25, 2015.

Bidgood, Jess. "Sunil Tripathi, Student at Brown, Is Found Dead." *New York Times*, April 25, 2013.

Bilton, Nick. "The Health Concerns in Wearable Tech." *New York Times*, March 18, 2015.

Boseley, Sarah. "Simon Singh Libel Case Dropped." *Guardian*, April 15, 2010.

Brandom, Russell. "The New York Times' Smartwatch Cancer Article Is Bad, and They Should Feel Bad." *Verge*, March 18, 2015. http://www.theverge.com/2015/3/18/8252087/cell-phones-cancer-risk-tumor-bilton-new-york-times. Accessed December 30, 2015.

British Chiropractic Association and Dr. Singh, England and Wales Court of Appeal (Civil Division) Decisions [2011] WLR 133, [2010] EWCA Civ. 350, [2011] 1 WLR 133.

Byers, Dylan. Twitter post, April 19, 2013, 1:57 a.m. https://twitter.com/DylanByers/status/325140977725616128.

Canby, Peter. "Fact-Checking at *The New Yorker*." In *The Art of Making Magazines: On Being an Editor and Other Views from the Industry*, ed. Victor S. Navasky and Evan Cornog. New York: Columbia University Press, 2012.

Carlson, Jen. "'Bachelor' Producer Publicly Shames Fellow Airline Passenger on Twitter." *LAist*, November 29, 2013. http://laist.com/2013/11/29/elan_gale_angry_notes.php. Accessed December 30, 2016.

"CNN Correction: Supreme Court Ruling." CNN. http://cnnpressroom.blogs.cnn.com/2012/06/28/cnn-correction/, June 28, 2012.

Coghian, Andy. "Simon Singh Wins Libel Battle Against Chiropractors." *New Scientist*, April 15, 2010.

Con Edison. Twitter post, October 29, 2012, 10:13 p.m. https://twitter.com/ConEdison/statuses/263116397238960128.

"Daniel Brooks Baer." U.S. Department of State. http://www.state.gov/r/pa/ei/biog/214014.htm. Accessed March 22, 2015.

"Defamation." Legal Information Institute, Cornell University Law School. https://www.law.cornell.edu/wex/defamation. Accessed June 22, 2015.

Editor's Note. *Vogue*, October 2012.

"Epic Note Passing Between Passengers Gets UGLY On U.S. Thanksgiving (TWEETS)." *Huffington Post Canada*, November 28, 2013. http://www.huffingtonpost.ca/2013/11/28/elan-gael-passenger-fight_n_4357360.html. Accessed December 30, 2015.

"Ethical Journalism: A Handbook of Values and Practices for the News and Editorial Departments." *New York Times*, September 2004.

Finkel, Michael. "Is Youssouf Malé a Slave?" *New York Times*, November 18, 2001.

Gertz v. Robert Welch, Inc., No. 72-617. 418 U.S. 323 (1974).

Goldstein, Tom. "We're Getting Wildly Differing Assessments." *SCOTUSblog*, July 7, 2012. http://www.scotusblog.com/2012/07/were-getting-wildly-differing-assessments/. Accessed December 30, 2015.

Griffen, Scott. "Out of Balance: Defamation Law in the European Union and Its Effects on Press Freedom." International Press Institute, July 2014.

"Ground Rules for Interviewing State Department Officials." U.S. Department of State. http://www.state.gov/r/pa/prs/17191.htm. Accessed June 22, 2015.

"Heed Their Rising Voices" (advertisement). *New York Times*, March 29, 1960.

Hogan, Beatrice. Interview with the author, February 20, 2015.

Holpuch, Amanda. "Hurricane Sandy Brings Storm of Fake News and Photos to New York." *Guardian*, October 30, 2012.

Kaczynski, Andrew. "Reports: Chechen Brothers—Not Missing Brown Student—Are Suspects." BuzzFeed, April 19, 2013. http://www.buzzfeed.com/andrewkaczynski/nbc-reports-overseas-figures-not-missing-brown-student-are-s#.ypx2ZoGLY. Accessed December 30, 2015.

"Keep Libel Laws Out of Science." Sense about Science. http://www.senseaboutscience.org/pages/keep-libel-laws-out-of-science.html. Accessed June 22, 2015.

LaFrance, Adrienne. Interview with the author, November 7, 2014.

Langer, Eli. "This Man Is Hilariously Live-Tweeting His Flight-and-Feud with the Woman in #7A." Storify. https://storify.com/EliLanger/this-man-is-hilariously-live-tweeting-his-flight-n. Accessed June 23, 2015.

Madrigal, Alexis. "#BostonBombing: The Anatomy of a Misinformation Disaster." *Atlantic*, April 19, 2013.

Martel, Frances. "News Organizations Retract Reports of Rep. Giffords' Death; She Is Alive." *Mediaite*, January 8, 2011. http://www.mediaite.com/tv/report-rep-gabrielle-giffords-passed-away-after-point-blank-shooting-in-tuscon/. Accessed December 30, 2015.

Masson v. New Yorker Magazine, Inc. No. 89-1799, 501 U.S. 496 (1991).

Masson v. New Yorker Magazine. Nos. 87-2665, 87-2700. 960 F.2d. (9th Cir. 1992).

McDermid, Brendan. "Con Edison Workers Trapped in New York Power Plant by Sandy: Reuters Witness." Reuters, October 29, 2012. http://www.reuters.com/article/us-storm-sandy-coned-idUSBRE89T03D20121030. Accessed January 25, 2016.

Mohney, Gillian. "Airplane 'Note War' Goes Viral on Twitter." *ABC News*, December 1, 2013.

Moran, Lee. "'Bachelor' Producer Elan Gale Gets into Air Rage Battle Aboard Delayed Flight on Thanksgiving," *Daily News*, December 3, 2013.

National Federation of Independent Business v. Sebelius. No. 11-393. 567 U.S. (2011).

National Weather Service. "Hurricane/Post-Tropical Cyclone Sandy, October 22–29, 2012." Department of Commerce. http://www.nws.noaa.gov/os/assessments/pdfs/Sandy13.pdf. Accessed June 23, 2015.

Neumann, Ross. Twitter post, April 19, 2013, 1:59 a.m. https://twitter.com/rossneumann/status/325141515108233216.

New York Times Co. v. L. B. Sullivan. No. 39. 376 U.S. 254 (1964).

O'Connell, Michael. "'Bachelor' Producer Achieves Twitter Celebrity after Thanksgiving Flight Altercation." *Hollywood Reporter*, November 11, 2013.

O'Neil, Lauren. "Bachelor Producer Elan Gale Live-Tweets Epic Feud with Rude Passenger." CBC, November 29, 2013. http://www.cbc.ca/newsblogs/yourcommunity/2013/11/bachelor-producer-elan-gale-live-tweets-epic-feud-with-rude-airline-passenger.html. Accessed December 30, 2015.

Ossola, Alexandra. "No, Wearable Electronics Are Not Like Cigarettes." *Popular Science*, March 18, 2015.

Palank, Jacqueline. "High Court Won't Take Up Scottie Pippen Defamation Suit." *Wall Street Journal*, June 16, 2014.

Pekarsky, Michelle. "Airline Passenger Exchanges Notes, Gets Slapped by Woman He Considered Rude to Flight Crew." Fox4KC, November 29, 2013. http://fox4kc.com/2013/11/29/airline-passenger-exchanges-notes-gets-slapped-by-woman-he-considered-rude-to-flight-crew/. Accessed December 30, 2015.

Pippen v. NBC Universal Media, LLC. No. 13-1355. 134 S.Ct. 2829 (2014).

"Publication: Copyright Infringement." *AP Stylebook Online.* 2015.

"Publication: Defamation." *AP Stylebook Online.* 2015.

"Publication: Privacy." *AP Stylebook Online.* 2015.

Shepard, Alicia. "NPR's Giffords Mistake: Re-Learning the Lesson of Checking Sources." *NPR Ombudsman,* January 11, 2011.

———. "On Deep Background." *AJR,* December 1994.

Shontell, Alyson. "An Incredible Note-Passing War Broke Out on a Thanksgiving Day Flight and Things Escalated Quickly." *Business Insider,* November 29, 2013.

Showler and Davidson v. Harper's Magazine. No. 06-7001. U.S. App LEXIS 7025 (10th Cir. 2007).

Silverman, Craig. "A Year Later, False Reports of Rep. Giffords' Death Still Reverberate for the Press." *Poynter,* January 8, 2012. http://www.poynter.org/news/mediawire/158541/a-year-later-false-reports-of-rep-giffords-death-still-reverberate-for-the-press/. Accessed December 30, 2015.

Sonderman, Jeff. "CNN, Fox News Err in Covering Supreme Court Health Care Ruling." *Poynter,* June 28, 2012. http://www.poynter.org/news/mediawire/179144/how-journalists-are-covering-todays-scotus-health-care-ruling/. Accessed December 30, 2015.

Stern, Joanna. "Why Elan Gale Made Up an Epic 'Note War' on a Thanksgiving Flight." *ABC News,* December 4, 2013.

Stockton, Nick. "The Times' Attack on Wearables Is an Attack on Science." *Wired,* March 18, 2015.

"Terror at the Marathon." *Boston Globe* Metro Special. http://www.bostonglobe.com/metro/specials/boston-marathon-explosions. Accessed June 23, 2015.

Van Meter, Jonathan. "Waiting in the Wings." *Vogue,* September 2012.

"The Winsted Wildman." Colebrook Historical Society. http://www.colebrookhistoricalsociety.org/PDF%20Images/The%20Winsted%20Wildman.pdf. Accessed June 23, 2015.

"Yellow Journalism." PBS, 1999. http://www.pbs.org/crucible/frames/_journalism.html. Accessed December 30, 2015.

Zarrell, Rachel. "This Epic Note-Passing War on a Delayed Flight Won Thanksgiving [Updated]." BuzzFeed, November 28, 2013. http://www.buzzfeed.com/rachelzarrell/this-epic-note-passing-war-on-a-delayed-flight-wins-thanksgi#.lnW27BvZR. Accessed December 30, 2015.

Zimmer, Carl. E-mail to the author, February 9, 2015.

CHAPTER TWO

Beers, Dan, Peter Kariene, and Brian Sacca. *Fact Checkers Unit (FCU)*. Directed by Dan Beers. 2007. New York: Moxie Pictures.

Cotts, Cynthia. Interview with the author, March 22, 2015.

Cummings, Corinne. Interview with the author, March 13, 2015.

Mailer, Norman. "Oswald in the U.S.S.R." *New Yorker*, April 10, 1995.

———. *Oswald's Tale: An American Mystery.* New York: Random House, 1995.

Rolzhausen, Yvonne. Interview with the author, March 3, 2015.

Schiller, Lawrence. www.lawrenceschiller.com.

"Sundance Film Festival Announces 2008 Short Film Program." *PR Newswire*, December 5, 2007. http://www.prnewswire.com/news-releases/sundance-film-festival-announces-2008-short-film-program-58596532.html. Accessed December 30, 2015.

CHAPTER THREE

Abdoh, Salar. Interview with the author, November 13, 2014.

Agish, Meral. Interview with the author, February 10, 2015.

Aikins, Ross. Interview with the author, February 2, 2015.

Alkon, Cheryl. Interview with the author, January 22, 2015.

Arratoon, Adrian. Interview with the author, February 3, 2015.

Attar, Robert. Interview with the author, February 13, 2015.

Bagley, Katherine. Interview with the author, January 6, 2015.

Banta, John. Interview with the author, March 19, 2015.

Bennett, Sid, Vaibhav Bhatt, and Charlie Foley. *Mermaids: The Body Found.* Directed by Sid Bennett. 2011. London: Darlow Smithson Productions.

Berger, Michele. E-mail to the author, March 18, 2015.

Bertsche, Rob. Interview with the author, March 25, 2015.

Bhatia, Rahul. Interview with the author, February 3, 2015.

Blanton, Riley. Interview with the author, March 5, 2015.

Bodin, Madeline. Interview with the author, February 5, 2015.

Brooks, Jillian. Interview with the author, February 4, 2015.

Canby, Peter, and Carolyn Kormann. Interview with the author, November 3, 2014.

CBSNews.com Staff. "Female Pilot Sues Over Muslim Garb." *60 Minutes*, January 17, 2002.

Ciarrocca, Michelle. Interview with the author, February 9, 2015.

Collazo, Julie Schwietert. E-mail to the author, February 8, 2015.

Condon, Emily. Interview with the author, February 18, 2015.

Conrad, Jennifer. E-mail to the author, February 18, 2015.

Cosier, Susan. Interview with the author, January 15, 2015.

Cotts, Cynthia. Interview with the author, March 22, 2015.

Cummings, Corinne. Interview with the author, March 13, 2015.

D'Anastasio, Cecilia. Interview with the author, March 9, 2015.

Dazell, Becky. Interview with the author, February 3, 2015.

Dillow, Clay. Interview with the author, January 6, 2015.

Discover Fact-Checking Guide (unpublished).

Dost, Stephen. Interview with the author, March 10, 2015.

"Eaten Alive." Snopes, December 7, 2014. http://www.snopes.com/info/news/eatenalive.asp. Accessed December 30, 2015.

Emig, Danielle. Interview with the author, February 9, 2015.

Esteves, Bernando. Interview with the author, February 4, 2015.

Finkbeiner, Ann. Interview with the author, January 12, 2015.

Fishman, Boris. Interview with the author, November 8, 2014.

George, Rose. Interview with the author, February 17, 2015.

Greenberg, Julia. Interview with the author, January 6, 2015.

Grunbaum, Mara. Interview with the author, February 16, 2015.

Harris, Michelle. Interview with the author, March 12, 2015.

Hermann, Todd, Paul Durbin, and Scott Wyerman. Interview with the author, April 7, 2015.

Hogan, Beatrice. Interview with the author, February 20, 2015.

Hunger, Bertolt. E-mail to the author, February 17, 2015.

Jameson, Daniel. Interview with the author, January 20, 2015.

Jones, Alice. Interview with the author, February 3, 2015.

Kachka, Boris. "Will Book Publishers Ever Start Fact-Checking? They're Already Starting." *Vulture*, June 23, 2015. http://www.vulture.com/2015/06/will-book-publishers-ever-start-fact-checking.html#. Accessed December 30, 2015.

Kaufman, Dan. Interview with the author, November 21, 2014.

Kralyevich, Vinnie. Interview with the author, March 11, 2015.

Krieger, Emily. Interview with the author, February 13, 2015.

Krogh, Ryan. Interview with the author, March 5, 2015.

LaFrance, Adrienne. Interview with the author, November 7, 2014.

Levitt, Aimee. Interview with the author, February 4, 2015.

Liguori, Rob. Interview with the author, November 16, 2015.

Maldonado, Cristina. Interview with the author, February 6, 2015.

"Manuscript Preparation." *The Chicago Manual of Style Online*. http://www.chicagomanualofstyle.org/qanda/data/faq/topics/ManuscriptPreparation/faq0006.html. Accessed June 22, 2015.

McClusky, Mark. Interview with the author, March 10, 2015.
McLaughlin, John. *Megalodon: The Monster Shark*. Directed by Doug Glover. North Hollywood: Pilgrim Studios, 2013.
McManus, Emily. Interview with the author, February 18, 2015.
"Megalodon: The Monster Shark Lives." Snopes, August 10, 2014. http://www.snopes.com/critters/malice/megalodon.asp. Accessed December 30, 2015.
Miguez, Luiza Machado. Interview with the author, March 6, 2015.
"A Million Little Lies." Smoking Gun, January 8, 2006. http://www.thesmokinggun.com/documents/celebrity/million-little-lies. Accessed January 2, 2016.
"Moment #18: Oprah Confronts James Frey." *The Oprah Winfrey Show*. 2006. http://www.oprah.com/own-tv-guide-magazines-top-25-best-oprah-show-moments/Moment-18-Oprah-Confronts-James-Frey-Video. Accessed January 2, 2016.
Murano, Edgard. Interview with the author, February 4, 2015.
Murphy, Kate. Interview with the author, March 4, 2015.
Muselmann, Jacob. Interview with the author, March 3, 2015.
O'Donnell, Nora. Interview with the author, April 1, 2015.
Ornes, Stephen. Interview with the author, February 5, 2015.
Palmer, Katie. Interview with the author, January 9, 2015.
Palus, Shannon. Interview with the author, January 6, 2015.
Pandell, Lexi. Interview with the author, February 6, 2015.
Parker, Ashley. "Pioneering Combat Pilot Persists in Rise from Arizona." *New York Times*, March 30, 2015.
Poe, Charles. Interview with the author, March 12, 2015.
Popular Science Fact-Checking Guide (unpublished).
"Proofreading." *The Chicago Manual of Style Online*. http://www.chicagomanualofstyle.org/tools_proof.html. Accessed June 22, 2015.
Rausch, Katherine. Interview with the author, January 21, 2015.
Redden, Molly. Interview with the author, January 27, 2015.
Reed, Jordan. Interview with the author, February 20, 2015.
Reed, Susan. Interview with the author, February 17, 2015.
Robb, Amanda. "A Fighter Pilot Takes the Fight to D.C.," *More*, April 2015.
Rojas-Burke, Joe. Interview with the author, February 11, 2015.
Rolzhausen, Yvonne. Interview with the author, March 3, 2015.
Rosolie, Paul. *Eaten Alive*. The Discovery Channel, 2014.
Rubin, Deborah. Interview with the author, February 17, 2015.
Ruiz, Matthew. Interview with the author, January 26, 2015.
Schaefer, Maximilian. Interview with the author, February 2, 2015.

Silverman, Craig. Interview with the author, September 30, 2014.
"Smith-Cantwell Amendment Lifting Abaya Requirement on American Servicewomen in Saudi Arabia Expected to Pass Senate Today." Maria Cantwell, U.S. Senator for Washington. http://www.cantwell.senate.gov/public/index.cfm/press-releases?ID=f3a35aff-4283-4793-8372-3e777e882d42&. Accessed June 22, 2015.
Smusiak, Cara. Interview with the author, February 10, 2015.
Southorn, Graham. Interview with the author, January 28, 2015.
Villani, Erika. Interview with the author, February 10, 2015.
Voosen, Paul. Interview with the author, February 2, 2015.
Wade, Lizzie. Interview with the author, January 15, 2015.
Waldman, Jonathan. Interview with the author, January 22, 2015.
Wiebe, Jamie. Interview with the author, January 15, 2015.
Williams, Stacie. Interview with the author, January 9, 2015.
Wojcicki, Ester. Interview with the author, March 5, 2015.
Zaleski, Luke. Interview with the author, March 4, 2015.
Zielinski, Sarah. Interview with the author, February 3, 2015.
Zimmer, Carl. E-mail to the author, February 9, 2015.
Zorich, Zach. Interview with the author, January 21, 2015.
Zweig, David. Interview with the author, February 9, 2015.

CHAPTER FOUR

Abdoh, Salar. Interview with the author, November 13, 2014.
Agish, Meral. Interview with the author, February 10, 2015.
Aikins, Ross. Interview with the author, February 2, 2015.
Alkon, Cheryl. Interview with the author, January 22, 2015.
"American Eel." The United States Fish and Wildlife Service. http://www.fws.gov/northeast/newsroom/pdf/Americaneel9.26.11.2.pdf. Accessed June 22, 2015.
"Anonymous Sources." *AP Stylebook Online*. 2015.
Arratoon, Adrian. Interview with the author, February 3, 2015.
Associated Press. *Manual de Estilo*. http://www.manualdeestiloap.com/.
Attar, Robert. Interview with the author, February 13, 2015.
Bagley, Katherine. Interview with the author, January 6, 2015.
Banta, John. Interview with the author, March 19, 2015.
Berger, Michele. E-mail to the author, March 18, 2015.
Bertsche, Rob. Interview with the author, March 25, 2015.
Bhatia, Rahul. Interview with the author, February 3, 2015.
Bissinger, Buzz. "Shattered Glass." *Vanity Fair*, September 1998.
Blanton, Riley. Interview with the author, March 5, 2015.

Bodin, Madeline. Interview with the author, February 5, 2015.
Boseley, Sarah. "Processed Meats Rank Alongside Smoking as Cancer Causes—WHO." *Guardian*, October 26, 2015.
Brooks, Jillian. Interview with the author, February 4, 2015.
Canby, Peter, and Carolyn Kormann. Interview with the author, November 3, 2014.
Ciarrocca, Michelle. Interview with the author, February 9, 2015.
Collazo, Julie Schwietert. E-mail to the author, February 8, 2015.
Condon, Emily. Interview with the author, February 18, 2015.
Conrad, Jennifer. E-mail to the author, February 18, 2015.
Cosier, Susan. Interview with the author, January 15, 2015.
Cotts, Cynthia. Interview with the author, March 22, 2015.
Cummings, Corinne. Interview with the author, March 13, 2015.
D'Anastasio, Cecilia. Interview with the author, March 9, 2015.
Dazell, Becky. Interview with the author, February 3, 2015.
Dillow, Clay. Interview with the author, January 6, 2015.
Discover Fact-Checking Guide (unpublished).
Dost, Stephen. Interview with the author, March 10, 2015.
Emig, Danielle. Interview with the author, February 9, 2015.
Epstein, Reid. "Alaska Election Offers Two Chances to Vote for Dan Sullivan." *Wall Street Journal*, August 12, 2014.
Esteves, Bernando. Interview with the author, February 4, 2015.
"Fact Sheet: Independent States in the World." U.S. Department of State. December 30, 2014. http://www.state.gov/s/inr/rls/4250.htm. Accessed January 2, 2016.
Finkbeiner, Ann. Interview with the author, January 12, 2015.
Fishman, Boris. Interview with the author, November 8, 2014.
Fortenbaugh, Robert. *The Nine Capitals of the United States*. New York: Maple Press Co., 1948. Reprinted at http://www.senate.gov/reference/reference_item/Nine_Capitals_of_the_United_States.htm. Accessed June 23, 2015.
Franklin, Tim, and Bill Adair. Interview with the author, October 30, 2015.
"Freshwater Eel." New York State Department of Environmental Conservation. http://www.dec.ny.gov/animals/85760.html. Accessed June 22, 2015.
George, Rose. Interview with the author, February 17, 2015.
Glass, Ira. "Mr. Daisey and the Apple Factory." *This American Life*. January 6, 2012. http://www.thisamericanlife.org/radio-archives/episode/454/mr-daisey-and-the-apple-factory. Accessed February 29, 2016.

Greenberg, Julia. Interview with the author, January 6, 2015.
"Growth in United Nations Membership, 1945–Present." United Nations. http://www.un.org/en/members/growth.shtml. Accessed June 22, 2015.
Grunbaum, Mara. Interview with the author, February 16, 2015.
Harris, Michelle. Interview with the author, March 12, 2015.
Hermann, Todd, Paul Durbin, and Scott Wyerman. Interview with the author, April 7, 2015.
Hogan, Beatrice. Interview with the author, February 20, 2015.
Hough, Andrew. "CNN Sorry Over Graphic Blunder That Uprooted London to Norfolk." *Telegraph*, February 3, 2012.
"How Many Countries are in the World?" *World Atlas*. http://www.worldatlas.com/nations.htm. Accessed June 22, 2015.
Hunger, Bertolt. E-mail to the author, February 17, 2015.
Hurst, Phoebe. "Sorry Everyone, Bacon Could Be as Bad for You as Cigarettes." *Munchies*, October 23, 2015. http://munchies.vice.com/articles/sorry-everyone-bacon-could-be-as-bad-for-you-as-cigarettes. Accessed January 2, 2016.
In re Stephen Randall Glass on Admission, S196374 State Bar Ct., No. 09-M-11736 (Cal. Jan. 27, 2014).
International Agency for Research on Cancer, "Agents Classified by the IARC Monographs, Volumes 1–114." http://monographs.iarc.fr/ENG/Classification/. Accessed November 5, 2015.
Irwig, Les, et al. "Chapter 18: Relative Risk, Relative and Absolute Risk Reduction, Number Needed to Treat and Confidence Intervals." In *Smart Health Choices: Making Sense of Health Advice*. London: Hammersmith Press, 2008.
Jameson, Daniel. Interview with the author, January 20, 2015.
Jones, Alice. Interview with the author, February 3, 2015.
Kaufman, Dan. Interview with the author, November 21, 2014.
Kralyevich, Vinnie. Interview with the author, March 11, 2015.
Krieger, Emily. Interview with the author, February 13, 2015.
Krogh, Ryan. Interview with the author, March 5, 2015.
LaFrance, Adrienne. Interview with the author, November 7, 2014.
Levitt, Aimee, Interview with the author, February 4, 2015.
Liguori, Rob. Interview with the author, November 16, 2015.
Maldonado, Cristina. Interview with the author, February 6, 2015.
McClusky, Mark. Interview with the author, March 10, 2015.
McManus, Emily. Interview with the author, February 18, 2015.
Miguez, Luiza Machado. Interview with the author, March 6, 2015.

Murano, Edgard. Interview with the author, February 4, 2015.
Murphy, Kate. Interview with the author, March 4, 2015.
Murphy, Mekado. "Werner Herzog Is Still Breaking the Rules." *New York Times*, July 1, 2007.
Muselmann, Jacob. Interview with the author, March 3, 2015.
O'Donnell, Nora. Interview with the author, April 1, 2015.
Ornes, Stephen. Interview with the author, February 5, 2015.
Palmer, Katie. Interview with the author, January 9, 2015.
Palus, Shannon. Interview with the author, January 6, 2015.
Pandell, Lexi. Interview with the author, February 6, 2015.
Poe, Charles. Interview with the author, March 12, 2015.
Popular Science Fact-Checking Guide (unpublished).
Rausch, Katherine. Interview with the author, January 21, 2015.
Redden, Molly. Interview with the author, January 27, 2015.
Reed, Jordan. Interview with the author, February 20, 2015.
Reed, Susan. Interview with the author, February 17, 2015.
"Regional Variations in Spanish Words Translated from English." Rennert. http://www.rennert.com/translations/resources/spanishvariations.htm. Accessed April 3, 2015.
Rojas-Burke, Joe. Interview with the author, February 11, 2015.
Rolzhausen, Yvonne. Interview with the author, March 3, 2015.
Rosin, Hanna. "Hello, My Name Is Stephen Glass, and I'm Sorry." *New Republic*, November 10, 2014.
———. Interview with the author, November 17, 2015.
Rubin, Deborah. Interview with the author, February 17, 2015.
Ruiz, Matthew. Interview with the author, January 26, 2015.
Schaefer, Maximilian. Interview with the author, February 2, 2015.
Schroeck, Eric. "Fox News *Again* Mislabels Vermont as New Hampshire," *Media Matters*, January 7, 2012.
Silverman, Craig. Interview with the author, September 30, 2014.
Smusiak, Cara. Interview with the author, February 10, 2015.
Somaiya, Ravi. "Stephen Glass Repays Harper's $10,000 for His Discredited Work." *New York Times*, October 16, 2015.
Southorn, Graham. Interview with the author, January 28, 2015.
Villani, Erika. Interview with the author, February 10, 2015.
Voosen, Paul. Interview with the author, February 2, 2015.
Wade, Lizzie. Interview with the author, January 15, 2015.
Waldman, Jonathan. Interview with the author, January 22, 2015.
Wiebe, Jamie. Interview with the author, January 15, 2015.
Williams, Stacie. Interview with the author, January 9, 2015.

Wohlsen, Marcus. "Inside Dropbox's Quest to Bury the Hard Drive." *Wired*, September 17, 2013.

Wojcicki, Ester. Interview with the author, March 5, 2015.

Yong, Ed. "Beefing with the World Health Organization's Cancer Warnings." *Atlantic*, October 26, 2015.

Zaleski, Luke. Interview with the author, March 4, 2015.

Zielinski, Sarah. Interview with the author, February 3, 2015.

Zimmer, Carl. E-mail to the author, February 9, 2015.

Zorich, Zach. Interview with the author, January 21, 2015.

Zweig, David. Interview with the author, February 9, 2015.

CHAPTER FIVE

"Advice on Predatory Journals and Publishers." Open Access at Manchester. http://www.openaccess.manchester.ac.uk/checkjournal/predatoryjournals/. Accessed June 23, 2015.

"Anonymous Sourcing." *NPR Ethics Handbook*. http://ethics.npr.org/tag/anonymity/. Accessed June 23, 2015.

Bartholomew, Robert. "Science for Sale: The Rise of Predatory Journals." *Journal of the Royal Society of Medicine* 107, no. 10 (October 2014): 384–85.

Beall, Jeffrey. "Beall's List: Potential, Possible, or Probable Predatory Scholarly Open-Access Publishers." *Scholarly Open Access*, November 5, 2015. http://scholarlyoa.com/publishers/. Accessed January 25, 2016.

Benedikt, Allison, and Hanna Rosin. "The Missing Men," *Slate*, December 2, 2014. http://www.slate.com/articles/double_x/doublex/2014/12/sabrina_rubin_erdely_uva_why_didn_t_a_rolling_stone_writer_talk_to_the_alleged.html. Accessed January 2, 2016.

Blanton, Riley. Interview with the author, March 5, 2015.

Brooke, Chris. "So Miracles DO Happen! As Flesh-Eating Bug Left Toddler at Death's Door, His Mother Turned to Prayer . . . and Just Look at Him Now." *Daily Mail*, June 10, 2013.

Canby, Peter. Interview with the author, November 3, 2014.

Clark, Jocalyn. "How to Avoid Predatory Journals—a Five Point Plan." *BMJ*, January 19, 2015. http://blogs.bmj.com/bmj/2015/01/19/jocalyn-clark-how-to-avoid-predatory-journals-a-five-point-plan/. Accessed January 2, 2016.

Coronel, Sheila, Steve Coll, and Derek Kravitz. "How Columbia Journalism School Conducted This Investigation." *Columbia Journalism Review*, April 5, 2015.

———. "*Rolling Stone* and UVA: The Columbia University Graduate School of Journalism Report." *Rolling Stone,* April 5, 2015.

———. "*Rolling Stone*'s Investigation: 'A Failure That Was Avoidable.'" *Columbia Journalism Review,* April 5, 2015.

Cotts, Cynthia. Interview with the author, March 22, 2015.

Daily Mail Reporter, "Women Are Too Shy to Break through the Glass Ceiling, Says Female Scientist." *Daily Mail,* August 21, 2008.

Editors. "How to Survive 10 Nightmare Scenarios." *Outside,* November 6, 2007.

Emig, Danielle. Interview with the author, February 9, 2015.

"Evaluating Web Pages: Questions to Consider: Categories." Cornell University Library. http://guides.library.cornell.edu/evaluating_Web_pages. Accessed June 23, 2015.

"Evaluating Web Sites: A Checklist." University Libraries. http://www.lib.umd.edu/binaries/content/assets/public/usereducation/evaluating-web-sites-checklist-form.pdf. Accessed June 23, 2015.

Finkel, Michael. "Is Youssouf Malé a Slave?" *New York Times,* November 18, 2001.

———. "The Strange and Curious Tale of the Last True Hermit." *GQ,* September 2014.

"Flip-Flops May 'Raise Risk of Skin Cancer.'" *Daily Mail,* June 13, 2008.

Getty Research Institute. getty.edu/research.

Google Scholar. https://scholar.google.com/.

Grunbaum, Mara. Interview with the author, February 16, 2015.

Hartley-Parkinson, Richard. "Woman, 63, 'Becomes PREGNANT in the Mouth' with Baby Squid after Eating Calamari." *Daily Mail,* June 15, 2012.

Hermann, Todd, Paul Durbin, and Scott Wyerman. Interview with the author, April 7, 2015.

Hickley, Matthew, and Jason Bennetto. "One Out of Every Five Killers Is an Immigrant." *Daily Mail,* August 30, 2009.

"How to Read and Review a Scientific Journal Article: Writing Summaries and Critiques." Duke University Writing Studio. http://twp.duke.edu/uploads/media_items/scientificarticlereview.original.pdf. Accessed June 23, 2015.

"How to Read a Scientific Paper." Purdue University Libraries. https://www.lib.purdue.edu/help/tutorials/scientific-paper. Accessed June 23, 2015.

"How to Search on Google." https://support.google.com/websearch/answer/134479?hl=en. Accessed June 23, 2015.

JSTOR. http://www.jstor.org/.

Kapoun, Jim. "Teaching Undergrads WEB Evaluation: A Guide for Library Instruction." *College & Research Libraries News*, July/August 1998, 522–23.

King, James. "My Year Ripping Off the Web with the Daily Mail Online." *Gawker*, March 4, 2015. http://tktk.gawker.com/my-year-ripping-off-the-web-with-the-daily-mail-online-1689453286. Accessed January 2, 2016.

Kinkela, David. *DDT and the American Century: Global Health, Environmental Politics, and the Pesticide That Changed the World.* Chapel Hill: University of North Carolina Press, 2011.

Kolata, Gina. "For Scientists, an Exploding World of Pseudo-Academia." *New York Times*, April 7, 2013.

Krogh, Ryan. Interview with the author, March 5, 2015.

Lurie, Peter, et al. "Comparison of Content of FDA Letters Not Approving Applications for New Drugs and Associated Public Announcements from Sponsors: Cross Sectional Study." *BMJ*, April 8, 2015. http://www.bmj.com/content/350/bmj.h2758. Accessed January 2, 2016.

"Maps." USA.gov. http://www.usa.gov/Topics/Maps.shtml. Accessed June 23, 2015.

Merriam-Webster's Geographical Dictionary. Merriam-Webster, 2007.

Nicholas, Sadie, Alison Smith-Squire, and Rebecca Wright. "We Know UFOs Do Exist—We've Seen Them!" *Daily Mail*, May 19, 2008.

Nijhuis, Michelle. "The Pocket Guide to Bullshit Prevention." *The Last Word on Nothing*, April 29, 2014. http://lastwordonnothing.com/2014/04/29/the-pocket-guide-to-bullshit-prevention. Accessed January 2, 2016.

"A Note to Our Readers." *Rolling Stone*, December 5, 2014.

Ornes, Stephen. Interview with the author, February 5, 2015.

———. "The Nobel Thieves." *Discover Magazine*, June 2007.

Penenberg, Adam. *NYU Journalism Handbook for Students: Ethics, Law and Good Practice.* Open Access License. http://journalism.nyu.edu/publishing/ethics-handbook/human-sources/. Accessed April 9, 2015.

PubMed Help. http://www.ncbi.nlm.nih.gov/books/NBK3827/#pubmedhelp.PubMed_Quick_Start.

PubMed. http://www.ncbi.nlm.nih.gov/pubmed.

Purugganan, Mary, and Jan Hewitt. "How to Read a Scientific Article." Cain Project in Engineering and Professional Communication. http://www.owlnet.rice.edu/~cainproj/courses/HowToReadSciArticle.pdf. Accessed June 3, 2015.

Roberts, Donald and Richard Tren. *The Excellent Powder: DDT's Political and Scientific History.* Indianapolis: Dog Ear Publishing, 2010.

Romenesko, Jim. "Daily Mail Slaps Motherboard Writer's Byline on Story, Apparently to Avoid Plagiarism Charges." JimRomenesko.com, April 17, 2015. http://jimromenesko.com/2015/04/17/daily-mail-slaps-motherboard-writers-byline-on-story-to-avoid-plagiarism-charges/. Accessed January 2, 2016.

Siegel, Robert. "Reading Scientific Papers." *The Vaccine Revolutions.* http://web.stanford.edu/~siegelr/readingsci.htm. Accessed June 23, 2015.

Sumner, Petroc, et al. "The Association between Exaggeration in Health Related Science News and Academic Press Releases: Retrospective Observational Study," *BMJ* December 10, 2014. http://www.bmj.com/content/349/bmj.g7015. Accessed January 2, 2016.

Sutherland, William, et al. "Policy: Twenty Tips for Interpreting Scientific Claims." *Nature,* November 20, 2013.

United States Board on Geographic Names. http://geonames.usgs.gov/. Accessed June 23, 2015.

Wemple, Erik. "The Full Demise of Rolling Stone's Rape Story." *Washington Post,* December 11, 2014.

"Writing the Scientific Paper." The Writing Studio, Colorado State. http://writing.colostate.edu/guides/guide.cfm?guideid=83. Accessed June 23, 2015.

Wurster, Charles F. *DDT Wars: Rescuing Our National Bird, Preventing Cancer, and Creating the Environmental Defense Fund.* New York: Oxford University Press, 2015.

CHAPTER SIX

Dropbox, https://www.dropbox.com/.

Fact-checker and researcher interviews with the author.

Hightail. https://www.hightail.com/.

"Stet," *Oxford Dictionaries.* http://www.oxforddictionaries.com/us/definition/american_english/stet. Accessed June 23, 2015.

CHAPTER SEVEN AND APPENDIX ONE ANSWER KEY

Borel, Brooke. "Better Know a Plague: Measles, Mumps, and Rubella." *Popular Science,* February 6, 2014.

Byrne, Joseph, ed. *Encyclopedia of Pestilence, Pandemics, and Plagues.* Vols. I and II. Westport, CT: Greenwood Press, 2009.

"CFR Launches Interactive Map Tracking Vaccine-Preventable Disease Outbreaks." Council on Foreign Relations, October 24, 2011.

http://www.cfr.org/pharmaceuticals-and-vaccines/cfr-launches-interactive-map-tracking-vaccine-preventable-disease-outbreaks/p26278. Accessed May 12, 2015.

Council on Foreign Relations. http://www.cfr.org/.

Doucleff, Michaeleen. "How Vaccine Fears Fueled the Resurgence of Preventable Disease." *NPR Shots*, January 25, 2014.

Drum, Kevin. "Map of the Day: The High Cost of Vaccine Hysteria." *Mother Jones*, January 20, 2014.

Dvorsky, George. "All of These Outbreaks Could Have Been Prevented with Vaccines." *io9*, January 21, 2014. http://io9.gizmodo.com/all-of-these-outbreaks-could-have-been-prevented-with-v-1505667747. Accessed January 3, 2016.

Farley, Tim. "A Butterfly Flaps Its Wings on Twitter, and a Vaccine Map Goes Viral." Skeptical Software Tools, https://skeptools.wordpress.com/2014/01/27/butterfly-flaps-wings-twitter-vaccine-map-viral-cfr-denialism/. Accessed May 12, 2015.

Haberman, Clyde. "A Discredited Vaccine Study's Continuing Impact on Public Health." *New York Times*, February 1, 2015.

Hiltzik, Michael. "The Toll of the Anti-Vaccination Movement, in One Devastating Map." *Los Angeles Times*, January 20, 2014. http://www.latimes.com/business/hiltzik/la-fi-mh-antivaccination-movement-20140120-story.html. Accessed February 18, 2016.

Koerth-Baker, Maggie. "Values and Vaccines." *Aeon*, February 16, 2016.

McCormick, Rich. "Map of Preventable Disease Outbreaks Shows the Influence of Anti-Vaccination Movements." *Verge*, January 21, 2014. http://www.theverge.com/2014/1/21/5329478/vaccine-preventable-disease-outbreaks-show-anti-vaccine-movement-influence. January 3, 2016.

"Measles." Mayo Clinic. http://www.mayoclinic.org/diseases-conditions/measles/basics/symptoms/con-20019675. Accessed May 12, 2015.

"Measles." World Health Organization. http://www.who.int/immunization/topics/measles/en/. Accessed May 12, 2015.

"Measles and Rubella." Centers for Disease Control and Prevention. http://www.cdc.gov/globalhealth/measles/. Accessed May 12, 2015.

"Measles Fact Sheet." World Health Organization. http://www.who.int/mediacentre/factsheets/fs286/en/. Accessed May 12, 2015.

"Measles, Mumps, and Rubella (MMR) Vaccine." Centers for Disease Control and Prevention. http://www.cdc.gov/vaccinesafety/Vaccines/MMR/. Accessed May 12, 2015.

"Measles (Rubeola)." Centers for Disease Control and Prevention. http://www.cdc.gov/measles/hcp/. Accessed May 12, 2015.

"Measles (Rubeola): Signs and Symptoms." Centers for Disease Control and Prevention. http://www.cdc.gov/measles/about/signs-symptoms.html. Accessed May 12, 2015.

"Measles Vaccination." Centers for Disease Control and Prevention. http://www.cdc.gov/measles/vaccination.html. Accessed May 12, 2015.

"MMR Vaccine and Autism." American Academy of Pediatrics. http://www2.aap.org/immunization/families/autismwakefield.html. Accessed May 12, 2015.

Mnookin, Seth. *The Panic Virus.* New York: Simon & Schuster, 2012.

"Mumps." Centers for Disease Control and Prevention. http://www.cdc.gov/mumps/ Accessed May 12, 2015.

"Mumps." World Health Organization. http://www.who.int/topics/mumps/en/. Accessed May 12, 2015.

Nyhan, Brendan, et al. "Effective Messages in Vaccine Promotion: A Randomized Trial." *Pediatrics* 133, no. 4 (April 2014).

Riggs, Mike. "This Map Shows the Extent of (Preventable) Whooping Cough Outbreaks." *The Wire,* January 22, 2014. http://www.thewire.com/national/2014/01/map-shows-extent-whooping-coughs-preventable-outbreaks/357255/. Accessed January 3, 2016.

"Rubella." Mayo Clinic. http://www.mayoclinic.org/diseasesconditions/rubella/basics/definition/con-20020067. Accessed May 12, 2015.

"Rubella." World Health Organization. http://www.who.int/mediacentre/factsheets/fs367/en/. Accessed May 12, 2015.

"Rubella (German Measles, Three-Day Measles)." Centers for Disease Control and Prevention: http://www.cdc.gov/rubella/. Accessed May 12, 2015.

"Salivary Gland Infections." U.S. National Library of Medicine MedlinePlus. http://www.nlm.nih.gov/medlineplus/ency/article/001041.htm. Accessed May 12, 2015.

Sherlick, Jeremy. E-mail to the author, February 6, 2014.

Taylor, Luke, et al. "Vaccines Are Not Associated with Autism: An Evidence-Based Meta-Analysis of Case-Control and Cohort Studies." *Vaccine* 32, no. 29 (2014): 3623–29.

"Transmission of Measles." Centers for Disease Control and Prevention. http://www.cdc.gov/measles/about/transmission.html. Accessed May 12, 2015.

"U.S. and World Population Clock." United States Census. http://www.census.gov/popclock/. Accessed May 12, 2015.

"Vaccine-Preventable Outbreaks." Council on Foreign Relations. http://www.cfr.org/interactives/GH_Vaccine_Map/#map. Accessed May 12, 2015.

"Vaccines." National Institute of Allergy and Infectious Diseases. http://www.niaid.nih.gov/topics/vaccines/understanding/pages/howwork.aspx. Accessed May 12, 2015.

"Vaccines: The Basics." Centers for Disease Control and Prevention. http://www.cdc.gov/vaccines/vpd-vac/vpd-vac-basics.htm. Accessed May 12, 2015.

Wallace, Amy. "An Epidemic of Fear: How Panicked Parents Skipping Shots Endanger Us All." *Wired*, October 19, 2009.

CONCLUSION

Adair, Bill. "Poynter to Hold Fact-Checking Summit in London." *Poynter*, April 4, 2014. http://www.poynter.org/news/mediawire/246261/poynter-to-hold-global-fact-checking-summit-in-london/. Accessed January 3, 2016.

"Alexa Report on Snopes.com." http://www.alexa.com/siteinfo/snopes.com. Accessed June 24, 2015.

"Antiviral: Here's What's Bullshit on the Internet This Week." *Gawker*.

Centers for Disease Control and Prevention. "Fast Stats: Immunization." http://www.cdc.gov/nchs/fastats/immunize.htm. Accessed June 22, 2015.

Dewey, Caitlin. "What Was Fake on the Internet This Week." WashingtonPost.com.

Dong, Xin Luna, et al. "Knowledge-Based Trust: Estimating the Trustworthiness of Web Sources." *Proceedings of the VLDB Endowment*, February 12, 2015.

Dzieza, Josh. "Website, Profiled: Why Are the Most Important People in Media Reading The Awl?" *Verge*, July 9, 2015. http://www.theverge.com/2015/7/9/8908279/the-awl-profile-choire-sicha-john-herrman-matt-buchanan. Accessed January 3, 2016.

Emergent. http://www.emergent.info/.

FactCheck. http://www.factcheck.org/.

Franklin, Tim, and Bill Adair. Interview with the author, October 30, 2015.

Kahan, Dan, et al. "Cultural Cognition of Scientific Consensus." *Journal of Risk Research*, September 10, 2010.

———. "Why We Are Poles Apart on Climate Change." *Nature News & Commentary*, August 15, 2012.

Lenz, Lyz. "Fact-Checking Grandma." *Aeon*, February 24, 2015. https://aeon.co/essays/should-you-fact-check-your-grandma-s-facebook-posts. Accessed February 18, 2016.

Lenz, Lyz. Interview with the author, March 12, 2015.

Leidig and Central European News Ltd. v. BuzzFeed Inc, 16-CV Complaint, United States District Court, Southern District of New York.

Lerner, Claire. E-mail to the author, October 28, 2015.

Meyer, Robinson. "Only You Can Stop Facebook Hoaxes." *Atlantic*, January 22, 2015.

Mikkelson, David. Interview with the author, March 5, 2015.

Mooney, Chris. "The Huge Implications of Google's Idea to Rank Sites Based on Their Accuracy." *Washington Post*, March 11, 2015.

O'Neil, Luke. "The Year We Broke the Internet," *Esquire*, December 23, 2013. http://www.esquire.com/news-politics/news/a23711/we-broke-the-internet/. Accessed January 20, 2016.

Oremus, Will. "Facebook Is Cracking Down on Viral Hoaxes. Really." *Slate*, January 20, 2015. http://www.slate.com/blogs/future_tense/2015/01/20/facebook_hoaxes_news_feed_changes_will_limit_false_news_stories.html. Accessed January 3, 2016.

Owens, Erich. "News Feed FYI: Showing Fewer Hoaxes." *Facebook Newsroom*, January 20, 2015. http://newsroom.fb.com/news/2015/01/news-feed-fyi-showing-fewer-hoaxes/. Accessed January 3, 2016.

PolitiFact. http://www.politifact.com/.

SciCheck. http://www.factcheck.org/scicheck/.

Silverman, Craig. Interview with the author, September 30, 2014.

Snopes. http://snopes.com/.

White, Alan, Tom Phillips, and Crag Silverman. "The King of Bullsh*t News." *BuzzFeed News*, April 24, 2015. http://www.buzzfeed.com/alanwhite/central-european-news#.gw6Qkm6op. Accessed January 3, 2016.

Witness Media Lab. https://lab.witness.org/.

Wohlsen, Marcus. "Stop the Lies: Facebook Will Soon Let You Flag Hoax Stories." *Wired*, January 1, 2015.

Index

Note: Page numbers followed by *f* indicate a figure.